LOVE
BETWEEN
MEN

LOVE

BETWEEN

MEN

*Enhancing Intimacy
and Keeping Your
Relationship Alive*

RIK ISENSEE

PRENTICE
HALL
PRESS

New York   London   Toronto   Sydney   Tokyo

Note: While the examples in this book are intended to reflect issues common to male couples, any resemblance to actual persons or situations is coincidental.

 Prentice Hall Press
15 Columbus Circle
New York, New York 10023

PRENTICE HALL PRESS and colophon are registered
trademarks of Simon & Schuster, Inc.

Library of Congress Cataloging-in-Publication Data

Isensee, Rik.
   Love between men : enhancing intimacy and keeping your
relationship alive / Rik Isensee.—1st ed.
       p.   cm.
   Includes bibliographical references.
   1. Gay male couples—United States.   2. Interpersonal relations.
I. Title.
HQ76.2.U5I84   1990
306.76′62—dc20   89-16253
                                                                   CIP

ISBN 0-13-540544-0

Designed by Stanley S. Drate/Folio Graphics Co. Inc.

Manufactured in the United States of America

10   9   8   7   6   5   4   3   2   1

First Edition

ACKNOWLEDGMENTS

I would like to thank the following friends and colleagues for their emotional support, valuable insights, and helpful criticism at numerous stages of this project: John A. Martin, Ph.D.; Diane Gray, Ph.D.; Carol Gerstein, MSW; and David Hedden.

I also want to thank the following couples, whose relationships inspired me, and who pointed out numerous ways to make my examples more realistic and relevant for other male couples: Gordon Murray, MFCC, and Paul Fresina; Mark Hall and John Dennis; Barry Savage, MA, and Tom Sinclair.

For their suggestions on handling AIDS-related issues: Helen Schietinger, RN, MFCC, consultant to the World Health Organization's Global Programme on AIDS, Geneva; Ken Pinhero, LCSW, coordinator of the AIDS Family Project, Operation Concern, San Francisco; and Michael D'Arata, RN, Planetree Model Unit, Pacific Presbyterian Medical Center, San Francisco.

For their comments and encouragement in response to an early draft: Drew Mattison, MSW, Ph.D.; Hillie Harned, Ph.D.; and Dennis DeBiase.

Thanks to my editor, Michael Moore, for his suggestions on tightening the manuscript, and for helping me clarify what I was trying to say; to my agent, Mitch Douglas at International Creative Management, whose vision and enthusiasm sustained me through a number of drafts; and to the male couples I've worked with over the years, who have demonstrated the depth of intimacy that is possible in love between men.

CONTENTS

P A R T

2

MAKING IT WORK

P A R T

3

SEEKING HELP 149

INTRODUCTION

Intimate contact—both sexual and emotional—is what many gay men are looking for in a relationship. Intimacy derives from a sense of mutual trust, and talking about how we feel enables trust to develop between us.

However, we face a number of challenges to our desire for intimacy with another man. Homophobia and discrimination make it dangerous to acknowledge same-sex attractions. We seldom see gay men portrayed realistically in the media and we've had few positive models for gay relationships. Our exposure to male couples living and coping together from day to day may be very limited. Without the encouragement from family and friends that heterosexual couples take for granted, we end up struggling on our own, with a scarcity of skills and support for handling the conflicts that inevitably arise in any relationship.

When we become involved with another man, we discover that our conditioning as males hasn't prepared us very well for the exchange of feelings that forms the basis for emotional intimacy. We've been taught to control or suppress our emotions, to the point where we may no longer be aware of how we feel. Having to hide our attractions while growing up may have left us mistrustful about disclosing our feelings to anyone. But if we don't say how we feel, it's hard to empathize with each other, so any serious conflict can lead to breaking off the relationship. What might have blossomed with the proper nurturing is allowed to wither, and we're left wondering whether love between men is even possible.

Though we risk alienation from our families, discrimination at work, and rejection by the surrounding community, many of us have reached out to one another to establish meaningful relationships. Through meeting the challenge of AIDS, we've learned a great deal about how to take care of ourselves as a community, and how to be more sensitive and responsive to one another's needs. Now many of us want to develop this same kind of emotional support with our partners.

In my work with male couples, we spend much of our time developing their ability to communicate clearly. I've been struck by how patterns of mutual antagonism give way to real understanding once partners work through past resentments and get to the core of their feelings toward each other. They often wonder why they couldn't have learned these skills a long time ago. Most of us never received much guidance from our families or at school about how to resolve interpersonal conflicts, much less what it takes to be involved in a relationship with another man. So I decided to put these ideas together in a form that male couples could use on their own.

Much of the skill-building approach I use in couples therapy is included in this book. It will take some work to translate these ideas into your own relationship—using a guide is not quite like having a therapist point out patterns between you, catch you when you interrupt each other, or help you listen when you're too upset to hear what your partner is saying. But you'll have some effective and practical tools to help you approach many of the problems you've been grappling with.

Every couple arrives at their own style for expressing affection and handling conflict; whatever works for you is what's important. But sometimes communication breaks down, and you're not sure how to reach out again. This book provides a model for working through conflicts and developing intimacy in gay relationships. You'll deepen your ability to express your feelings and empathize with your partner. Through detailed examples of issues common to male couples, you'll be able to identify patterns and solve most of the problems that arise between you.

When you first get to know someone, you may be attracted sexually and stimulated by common interests. Over time, an intimate connection evolves from your willingness to say what you think and how you feel. Revealing yourself is a great gift—as you struggle together, without having to pretend or hide your feelings, you come to love and appreciate each other as you really are.

That's the level of closeness I see develop between the men I work with, and that's what I hope this book can help you achieve in your own relationship.

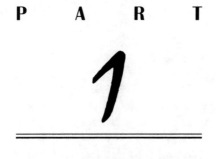

P   A   R   T

1

RESOLVING
CONFLICTS

Everything that rises must converge.
—TEILHARD DE CHARDIN

1

Dynamics in Gay Relationships

What is unique about gay male relationships? How we relate to one another is influenced not only by our emotional and sexual attraction for other men but also by how we've been socialized as males in a homophobic society. Homophobia isolates us, and male conditioning inhibits our awareness of feelings. Recognizing how these influences operate in our own relationships will help us challenge and overcome our isolation, and provide us the support we need to form an intimate bond with another man.

Internalized Homophobia

Whenever a group is discriminated against, its members may internalize a negative self-image. Most ethnic minorities have their own families and communities for support, but gay men are usually raised with the same prejudices about homosexuality as the surrounding culture. As boys, it may have felt threatening even to wonder whether we were gay, because our very willingness to consider the possibility implied that we were. Many of us spent much of our adolescence denying that we were attracted to other males, or trying to hide any indication that we were interested in same-sex relationships. We feared that if people knew what we were really like, they would reject us. Some men

3

deny their sexual orientation well into adulthood, assuming they'll eventually outgrow homosexual attractions.

Many of us have felt humiliated by our fathers, brothers, and other males for not conforming to masculine stereotypes. Depending on whether we could pass as heterosexual, we may have experienced varying degrees of harassment, from verbal taunts to physical and sexual abuse. For those of us who escaped actual assault, the threat of discovery was always with us. Though our invisibility protected us, it also contributed to our isolation.

We are probably most vilified by other men who have homosexual attractions but are so repulsed by the possibility of being gay that they project their feelings onto us. We become a container, in a sense, for their own repressed desires, and the recipients of their revulsion. This can be seen in extreme cases in violent attacks against gay men, but in more subtle forms it permeates our interaction with other males. The horror of being linked with homosexuality keeps men and boys from expressing vulnerability or affection, especially to one another.

With few positive models for gay relationships (or even of men nurturing one another), we're left with negative images from the media, or sometimes with no information at all. Homophobia creates a cycle of isolation, which tends to reinforce itself. Hiding our feelings from our friends may have led to furtive sexual encounters with strangers, which only reinforced our suspicion that gay relationships can't last. Cut off from a community of support, homophobia becomes a self-fulfilling prophecy: we end up internalizing the negative self-image that we feared was the fate of the "lonely homosexual."

Even if we consciously reject the irrational nature of the prejudice directed against us, we still have to cope with a hostile culture. Many of us developed various survival strategies: being secretive, pretending, and withdrawing from peer activities. It's natural that we would feel cautious about being emotionally vulnerable, since we learned it wasn't safe to disclose our innermost thoughts and desires. But some of these strategies can interfere with our adult desires for intimacy.

*　*　*

Male Socialization

There are certain needs that must be tended to in any relationship: basic physical requirements, such as food, clothing, and a place to live; and emotional needs, such as warmth, sex, and affection. In traditional heterosexual couples, these tasks have often been divided between the sexes: the wife was expected to nurture her husband and children, and put the needs of her family before her own; the husband solved problems involving manual dexterity and technical skill, earned a living, and initiated sex. Both roles include positive qualities, but we've been limited by the assignment of various human capacities to one sex or the other.

Although many gay men (and some heterosexual couples) reject these stereotypes of what it means to be "masculine" or "feminine," our conditioning as males can still influence how we relate to each other. For example, some research indicates that men tend to disclose less about themselves than women do, and both sexes reveal more personal information to women than they do to men.[1] Socialized to be analytical and critical, each man in a male couple may be so focused on his own independence that neither partner is oriented toward the emotional needs of their relationship. Unaccustomed to disclosing their feelings or listening to others, they may withdraw emotionally, or end up in competitive arguments over who's "right," rather than saying how they feel.

By understanding how we've been conditioned by these roles, we can balance traditional male abilities with skills associated with female sex roles: disclosing our feelings, listening to our partner, and developing an intuitive sense for the emotional needs of our relationship.

Influences of the Gay Subculture

While some men fall in love with their best friends in their home towns or when they go away to college, many gay men eventually gravitate to urban centers large enough to support a variety of settings where we can meet each other without fear of harassment.

The development of the post-Stonewall phase of gay liberation coincided with the sexual revolution, which led to a lot of sexual adventurousness among urban gay men in the 1970s. With no fear of pregnancy, and with both partners socialized to take the sexual initiative, there were few brakes on pursuing sexual contacts. Casual sex, combined with men's tendency not to reveal much about themselves, helped create an unspoken norm whereby gay men slept together without saying much about their expectations for the future.

The onslaught of AIDS has had a profound influence on our sexuality. Negotiating safer sex has required us to talk about our preferences and feelings. Though safe sex needn't preclude casual encounters, many of us have also begun to explore what we want from longer-term relationships. These explorations certainly took place before AIDS, as well, but our community's response to the epidemic has altered our social landscape considerably.

Ambiguity in Gay Relationships

Everyone has gradations of intimacy, from acquaintances to closer friends and lovers. Gay men don't have the markers of engagement, marriage, and pregnancy that characterize the bond between heterosexual couples. This lack of socially recognized status can be a source of ambiguity in our relationships—are we friends, occasional sexual partners, or lovers?

Though we don't need to follow heterosexual models in forming our own relationships, this ambiguity becomes problematic when it interferes with the expression of feelings. You may feel attracted sexually without having any idea as to whether you'll find yourselves compatible in other ways. If you have sex before you become emotionally involved, it can be confusing trying to figure out what else you want from each other. You may end up sleeping together once or twice, and then feel awkward trying to redefine the relationship.

Neither of you may be ready to make the commitment that continued sexual involvement might imply, but instead of dealing with that uncertainty by talking about options and expectations, it may seem easier not to see each other. Not every relationship has to last forever in order for us to get some value from it, but if you had more in mind than just recreational sex, you can end up feeling seduced and abandoned.

Some men are scared off by the intensity of their initial involvement. If you're not sure how you feel, you may hesitate to become involved emotionally. But you don't have to know what you want in the very beginning. After seeing each other for a while, you may need some distance in order to sort through your feelings. What may simply be a desire on the part of one man to reclaim himself may be misinterpreted by the other as a lack of interest in building a relationship. You can avoid this misunderstanding by talking about your need for time apart, while still affirming your interest in getting to know each other.

You can be clear about what you want at the moment, even if that involves a limit to the degree of emotional or sexual involvement you're interested in. You may feel vulnerable saying how you feel, especially when you're first getting to know each other, but being honest about your feelings increases your capacity for intimacy in the future.

Entering a Relationship

We enter a relationship with the reasonable hope that we'll meet our desires for companionship and sexual fulfillment, and we look forward to mutual growth. In the beginning, we go out of our way to accommodate each other—pleasing our partner pleases us; our love far outweighs any "petty" annoyances. Though the feelings of closeness that arise from our initial attraction are often gained by submerging differences, this "blending" stage forges a bond that may be able to withstand our desire to differentiate ourselves later.[2]

After a while, being on one's best behavior becomes a strain, and conflicts surface. The first major disagreement can lead to a premature breakup, or be so unsettling that we develop unspoken agreements not to touch on certain topics. But avoidance of conflict restricts the areas in which we interact, and decreases feelings of closeness. Our attempt to avoid confrontation actually increases the risk of conflict boiling over in the future, because we're not really working through our problems.

Dealing with conflict feels threatening because we're not sure how to talk about problems without making the situation worse. But *not* talking about how we feel leads to increasing distance in the relationship. So how can we approach conflicts with more confidence that we'll be able to resolve them?

Approaching Conflict

Conflict in relationships is inevitable. It's how we deal with conflict that determines whether our relationship is damaged or strengthened. If we anticipate conflict, we won't feel so overwhelmed when we encounter differences.

Conflict is healthy. Differences exist, whether we deal with them or not, and when we resolve them successfully, we feel closer. When acknowledging differences feels too threatening, intimacy wanes. It's by revealing who we really are, rather than projecting an image of how we'd like to be seen, that we continue to grow in our relationships.

Changes are inevitable as you grow older and your relationship develops—you have new career opportunities and financial obligations; outside interests and friendship networks shift; health may become an issue; your level of sexual involvement changes; and what you want from your relationship may alter over the years. You may wonder at times whether you'll be able to adjust successfully.

Maintaining a sense of yourself as an individual while still affirming the importance of your relationship is a significant task for any member of a couple. Men are socialized to function independently, so a male couple may have a difficult time finding the balance of "Who am I, who are you, and who are we together?" A sense of self allows a genuine exchange between you and your partner. You can't really feel close unless you experience yourself as a separate individual—otherwise, there's no "you" to appreciate the closeness. Similarly, taking your relationship into consideration (not just your own personal desires) allows you to weather the differences that inevitably arise.

You may grant that conflict is inevitable while still being skeptical about whether it's all that healthy. We need a way to talk about problems, instead of arguing and then withdrawing. In the rest of Part I we'll look at improving your ability to empathize, express your feelings, and avoid the pitfalls that commonly escalate conflict. Naturally, there may be times when you're too upset to remember any of these skills, and you end up in arguments and withdraw for a while anyway. But instead of ignoring the conflict and letting it build up again, you'll learn how to approach each other to work through your differences.

2

Empathic Listening

*L*istening is an essential skill for communicating clearly and developing empathy. When you listen to your partner and identify with his feelings, you help him get in touch with what's really bothering him. This increases his ability to listen to you. Once you both feel understood, it's easier to identify the true nature of your conflict and to think more clearly about how you want to solve a problem.

Misconceptions About Listening

People often say "He never listens to me," when what they really mean is "He doesn't agree with me, comply with what I want, or do what I suggest." In common speech, we confuse listening with agreement or compliance, so when we're upset with each other we may feel some resistance to hearing what the other person has to say.

Men often argue about ideas, rather than talking about feelings. Disputing ideas can inhibit your awareness of what's really at stake for you. When you look for logical contradictions in order to counter each other's feelings, you're not really listening. This is a "logical" mistake, if you will—emotions don't generally respond to logic. Feelings simply press for recognition, and often shift as soon as they're acknowledged.

Understanding doesn't equal agreement, but accurate listening helps you understand each other's point of view, so you can both clearly state what your conflict is about. You may still need to work on solving it, but your ability to find a mutually acceptable solution will be greatly improved by clarifying your differences.

Defensiveness

When your partner is angry with you, it may be difficult to keep still while he expresses his feelings. But when you're preoccupied with defending yourself, you stop listening. You may try to convince him there's really no reason to be upset, by any of the following means:

1. Giving excuses—"If only you knew why I was late, you wouldn't be mad at me."
2. Arguing about the facts—"It was 8:15, not 9:15, so you have no reason to be upset."
3. Offering advice—"Why don't you just quit your job and stop complaining."
4. Reassurance—"Everything will be all right, so stop feeling bad."
5. Countercomplaint—"I haven't seen you lift a finger, so you're one to talk."
6. Analyzing—"You're too dependent."

A defensive response is basically an attempt to get your partner to stop feeling, so you won't feel blamed. But interrupting your partner and trying to talk him out of his feelings tends to escalate a conflict, because neither of you feels heard. Just because he's upset doesn't mean you have to defend yourself, or try to make him feel better. He may just want to let you know how he feels, so there's really no need to do anything except listen. Once he feels understood, it will be easier for him to listen to you.

Likewise, if you're upset with your partner and he becomes defensive, he probably feels blamed, so you can back off and listen to him. Listening slows down your interaction so you both get a chance to say how you feel. Neither of you feels discounted as you clarify your problem. Instead of blaming each other, you're ready to work on solving the conflict.

Of course you're likely to feel defensive when your partner's angry with you—no one likes to feel blamed—so you're tempted to argue why you're not at fault. It helps to talk *about* your defensiveness, instead of just defending yourself by giving excuses, making countercomplaints, and so on. If you say "This is hard for me to hear. I'm feeling defensive right now," your partner may be able to back off and listen to you. Toward the end of this chapter we'll talk about how to handle arguments that escalate because you're both so upset that neither of you is able to listen.

How to Listen

Listening seems quite simple and passive, yet it can be a powerfully active process. It takes a lot of concentration to listen accurately, especially when your partner is upset with you.

Paying Attention
The first type of listening is mostly nonverbal: you simply pay close attention to what your partner says. It consists of eye contact, nods, an occasional "mm hmm," and open body language: facing him, you lean slightly forward, your arms and legs uncrossed. Most of us already do this whenever we listen tosomeone attentively, though we may not be consciously aware of it.

The closer attention you pay him, the quieter you become yourself. Since he's able to explain how he feels without being interrupted, your partner will have the sense that he's really getting through to you. If he's upset with you, he may need more acknowledgment that you've understood what he's upset about. This brings us to the next type of listening.

Paraphrasing
Paraphrasing consists of telling your partner, in your own words, what you heard. For the moment, you don't have to answer him or justify yourself; just say what you understood. Once he feels heard, it will be easier for him to listen to you. Knowing you'll have a chance to explain your side of the story later can help you listen without becoming defensive.

Paraphrasing can feel somewhat artificial at first, especially for couples who have their own shortcuts in communication. But however intuitive they might feel when they're doing well together, most couples have a great capacity for distortion when they're upset with each other. You can begin your feedback with something like "Let me see if I've got this right." Your tone of voice often has more impact than the actual words you use, so try to say what you've understood as fairly as possible, without being sarcastic or exaggerating your partner's point of view. Paraphrasing also allows him to modify or emphasize what he means. Don't argue about whether he really said what you understood. If it's not what he meant, this is simply an opportunity for him to clarify it for you.

Let's look at the following interaction to see how a defensive response leads to an escalating dispute. Then we'll illustrate how paraphrasing can help both partners feel understood.

Steve and Randy have planned to go to a concert at 8:00 P.M. Steve had dinner ready at 6:00, but Randy still hasn't gotten home by 7:15. Steve is about to leave when Randy rushes in.

RANDY: I'm home! Are you all set?

STEVE: You're late!

RANDY: I'm not late. [Randy argues about the facts.]

STEVE: It's nearly 7:30!

RANDY: We have plenty of time to get to the concert. [He tries to reassure Steve.]

STEVE: I had dinner ready at six o'clock.

RANDY: So why didn't you eat, then? [Randy feels blamed, and offers advice.]

STEVE: I was waiting for you.

RANDY: I didn't ask you to wait. [Randy tries to excuse his behavior and convince Steve he has no reason to be upset, because he never agreed to be home by 6:00.]

STEVE: Where were you, anyway? Out cruising the park? [Because Steve remains unacknowledged, he escalates.]

RANDY: I might as well have been, if this is what I have to come home to. [Randy counterattacks.]

STEVE: If you had any consideration, you would have at least called. [Steve implies Randy is inconsiderate.]

RANDY: I don't have to answer to you. [Randy reacts defensively to being called inconsiderate.]

STEVE: Yeah, well to hell with you! [Steve is furious, and escalates to demonstrate his hurt and sense of betrayal.]

Let's stop here and look at what just happened. Because they weren't really listening to each other, both partners felt undermined and devalued: Steve felt unappreciated for having made a nice dinner, and Randy felt unjustly accused. Since neither felt acknowledged, they escalated with most of the defensive reactions listed above, which made it even less likely that either would be able to listen.

Let's run through this again, with Randy paraphrasing Steve's concerns.

RANDY: I'm home! Are you all set?

STEVE: You're late!

RANDY: I'm late? [By repeating Steve's accusation as a question, he solicits more information.]

STEVE: I had dinner ready at six o'clock!

RANDY [looking at the table setting]: Oh, you fixed dinner. [Randy recognizes Steve's assumption that they would have dinner together.]

STEVE: Yeah, I thought we were going to eat before we went to the concert. [Because he has been acknowledged, he says more about his own assumption, rather than grilling Randy about where he was.]

RANDY: I got hung up at work. [Randy explains what held him up.]

STEVE: I wish you'd have called. [Steve says what he wants, rather than accusing Randy of being inconsiderate.]

RANDY: I'm sorry, I just assumed you'd go ahead and eat. [Randy apologizes, and says more about his assumption.]

STEVE: It wasn't so much that; I was worried that something happened to you. [Because Randy has made an effort to understand him, Steve says he was worried.]

Instead of damaging their relationship, Randy's willingness to listen to Steve and paraphrase him helped Steve get in touch with his underlying concern. Of course, they could have their initial quarrel, separate for a while, and then come back to listen to each other once they've had a chance to cool off. We'll look at this interaction again toward the end of this chapter.

Reflecting Feelings[1]

The third type of listening reflects what you imagine your partner is feeling. This isn't mind reading or psychoanalyzing; don't try to tell him what he's "really" feeling. It's simply a way to find out if you understand how he feels.

We often reflect feelings with friends who have just told us about some painful experience: "God, how awful!" "What a disappointment." When it's clear that you understand your partner, he can elaborate on how something has affected him, what it reminds him of, and what he hopes for in the future. Reflecting feelings helps him identify how he feels, and it also increases your own ability to empathize with him.

Empathy is the ability to put yourself in your partner's place and imagine how you'd feel if you had the same experience. Observe his body posture; listen to his voice; look at his eyes. Say what you imagine he might be feeling. It's not essential that you're "right"; your concern and effort to understand him will help him figure out how he feels.

For example, Scott tells Bill that Lenny, his former lover, is coming to town, and he wants to take him up to the mountains for the weekend.

BILL: That sounds like fun—I'll see if I can get Friday afternoon off so we can leave early.

SCOTT: Well, actually, I was hoping to spend some time with him by myself.

BILL: Oh. So, uh, you figure I'd be in the way? [Bill reflects Scott's concern.]

SCOTT: No, we just haven't seen each other in a long time. [He pauses, sensing that Bill may feel jealous, and tries to reflect Bill's feelings.] You think I'm trying to get something going again with Lenny?

BILL: It crossed my mind.

SCOTT: Well, I'm not. But it sounds like you're feeling left out, huh? [Scott reflects how he imagines Bill is feeling.]

BILL: Yeah, I guess, and a little jealous. [Because Scott was sensitive to his feelings, Bill admits he's jealous.]

By reflecting his feelings, Scott can reassure Bill about his caring for him. They can explore ways to spend time with friends as a couple, and also negotiate their desire for separate friend-ships.

Obviously, it's easier to be empathic if you're not preoccupied with defending yourself. When your partner's upset with you, it's difficult to step back and consider what's going on with him. But if you counter his complaint with one of your own without acknowledging him first, he's likely to polarize with you, and the conflict escalates. Empathizing with him will help him feel under-stood and increase his ability to listen to you.

Listening for Positive Intent

Positive intent is the wish for better relations that lies behind many hostile interactions. Hurtful statements often arise from a desire to demonstrate one's own pain. The reason two people have the capacity to hurt each other is usually that they care for each other. Behind the expression of pain there's a wish that things could be different.

For example, think of someone you were upset with in the past. What were your hopes about the relationship that weren't fulfilled? You may have wished he'd understood you, expressed his caring, or been more responsive. These wishes are the posi-tive intent behind the hurt.

Hostility often results from feeling threatened by the potential loss of your relationship. Yet attacking each other is likely to make your worst fears come true. When you're able to acknowl-edge your desire for better relations, you're more likely to enlist your partner's cooperation in finding a solution that takes you both into consideration.

You can use your own feelings as a clue to what your partner may feel, since we tend to elicit in others feelings that we experience ourselves. If you feel hurt, he probably does too, even if you don't think it's justified. You don't need to justify feelings through blame or logic. Mostly you just need to be heard and feel understood. You don't always need to state your partner's posi-tive intent; sometimes it's enough to realize that you feel the same way: "I wish things were going better, and he probably does too." This recognition helps you feel less defensive, so you can empathize with the desire for improved relations underlying his hostility, instead of retaliating. In the following example we can see how recognizing the positive intent behind a defensive re-sponse can keep the conflict from escalating.

Greg comes home and opens the refrigerator, then slams the door. "There's never anything to eat around here!" he exclaims, and rummages through the cupboard.

Kevin, assuming that Greg is blaming him, retorts, "You expect it's going to walk in the door and stick itself in the fridge?"

GREG: It was your turn to go shopping.
KEVIN: I had to work late every night this week!
GREG: Green's is open till midnight.
KEVIN: So? Would it kill you to pick up a few things yourself?
GREG: Would it kill you to follow through on our agreements?
KEVIN: Get off my back.

At this point Greg realizes that Kevin feels too defensive to listen to his concerns. He considers the positive intent behind Kevin's defensiveness: he's under pressure at work, and probably wishes Greg could be more supportive.

GREG: You wish I'd give you a little slack.
KEVIN: Yeah! We're on a deadline, and I've been eating on the run. My brain's fried when I get home.
GREG: Shopping's probably the last thing on your mind.
KEVIN: To say the least.

Once Kevin has been acknowledged, Greg says more about what he'd like: "I understand what you're going through, but I've been busy too. So how can we keep from starving in the meantime?"

Because Greg recognizes Kevin's defensiveness, he is able to step back for a moment to reflect the positive intent behind Kevin's hostility: "You wish I'd give you a little slack." In turn, Kevin lets him know that he was so preoccupied with his deadline, he never gave a thought to grocery shopping. Greg empathizes with the pressure Kevin has been under at work. Rather than blaming, Greg invites Kevin to help him solve the problem of keeping enough food in the house, even when they're both very busy.

*   *   *

What If You're Too Upset to Listen?

It's normal in any relationship to have times when you rub each other the wrong way. You may not be in a great mood, your signals get crossed, and you don't have the patience to listen very well and sort through your feelings. The skills outlined here are not intended as an ideal to live up to, but as tools you can use when you get bogged down. Listening can keep you from escalating in the first place; but if you have an argument anyway, listening can help you work through your conflict once you've had the chance to cool off.

When you're both too upset to listen, you'll probably go through the following cycle: you have a quarrel, in which neither of you feels heard; you withdraw for a while; and then you try to make up in some fashion.

The Quarrel

It's very difficult to listen when you're upset. Both of you feel frustrated because neither feels heard. You may exaggerate your points, dredge up past conflicts, and say spiteful things to demonstrate your hurt. Knowing that this is what people do when they're not getting through to each other can help you ride out the storm. It doesn't have to be the end of the world (or the end of your relationship) just because you get angry with each other.

Withdrawal

When you've had a bitter quarrel, you will probably withdraw for a while to cool off. Sometimes one partner will leave the scene to demonstrate how fed up he is, and the other will feel abandoned. Since it's likely at some point that one or both of you will withdraw, it helps to predict this by agreeing on a way to call time out. (We'll go into this more in chapters 4 and 14.)

One reason for withdrawing after a fight is the fear that talking about what happened will just start the quarrel all over again. Withdrawal is one strategy for keeping out of each other's way for a while. But many couples don't ever make up, because they're not sure how to approach each other without getting into another argument, or they don't want to appear to be giving in. After feeling tense for a few days, they try to act as if nothing ever happened, and hope it will all blow over.

Making Up

Ignoring the conflict leads to increasing distance, and it's likely that the same issues will build up again. Though you both probably said a lot of foolish things, the quarrel may have revealed some hidden resentments that should be discussed. So you need a way to get back together and talk about what happened.

You can approach your partner to see whether he's ready to talk about your argument. Disclosing the hurt and fear behind your anger will help you listen to each other. Acknowledging your own part in escalating the conflict can also help. Did you give advice, make excuses, or accuse him? If you can acknowledge some points he made that you agree with, he may be willing to consider some of the points you made, too.

Our example with Steve and Randy in the section on paraphrasing showed how things might have turned out if they had been able to listen to each other. But they may have been too upset to listen right then, so let's look at how they could have talked about their quarrel the following day.

RANDY: Could we talk about what happened last night?

STEVE: I don't know; can we?

RANDY: I'd like to try.

STEVE: I'm still feeling pretty sore.

RANDY: I know I was being defensive last night. I guess it was hard for me to hear your disappointment about dinner. [He takes an initial stab at owning up to his part in the argument. Steve nods and listens, still a little wary.] I know you went out of your way to make a nice meal, and I appreciate that. [He acknowledges Steve's effort.]

STEVE: Well, thanks. I should have realized you were held up.

RANDY: I could have called. I was so rushed at work, it didn't even occur to me. [He acknowledges Steve's wish that he had called, without needling Steve for implying he was inconsiderate.]

STEVE: I never gave you a chance to explain what happened. I was all over your case as soon as you walked through the door. [Steve is willing to admit that he contributed to their difficulty, too.]

RANDY: I didn't mean it when I said you're not worth coming home to. I was just mad. [He apologizes for his hurtful remark.]

STEVE: I'm sure accusing you of stopping by the park didn't help any. [Steve acknowledges his part in provoking Randy.]

Randy listens, without saying anything. Then Steve says, "I was just worried something had happened to you, and I guess a little scared that I *wasn't* worth coming home to," disclosing the fear behind his anger.

Because Randy acknowledges his part in the dispute, it was easier for Steve to say he felt concerned and expose his underlying fear. Randy can reassure him, and they can go on to discuss their expectations for checking in with each other in the future.

Listening Practice

You may not be able to listen, much less solve the problem, until you've had a chance to express your frustration. But it's hard to express your feelings without interrupting each other when you're both upset. It takes some practice (and patience!) to use these methods effectively. Practice can make these skills more available when you need them.

It's easier to learn new skills when you're not dealing with emotionally laden issues. Before dealing with actual conflicts in your relationship, you might want to try these brief exercises:

First, take turns paying attention to each other. When you listen to your partner, it may feel odd not to say anything in response. Questions may occur to you that you'd like to have clarified, or challenges to his assumptions may spring to mind. For the moment, see what it's like to listen. Without meeting any resistance, he may fill in some of these gaps himself. When he listens to you, you'll see how satisfying it can be to have someone pay you such close, mostly silent attention.

After paying attention, look at each of the following statements and see if you can come up with your own paraphrase, reflection of feelings, and what you think might be the underlying positive intent.

Practice 1. Jack says, "This apartment is such a pigsty!" A defensive response might be a countercomplaint: "I haven't seen you doing much to keep it clean." Such a statement could easily lead to an argument. Let's look at possible responses that would acknowledge his concern.

PAYING ATTENTION: You may not need to say much in response. If you look at him and nod, he's likely to say more about his desire for a clean apartment.

PARAPHRASE: This might be a simple acknowledgment: "It's really a mess."

REFLECTING FEELINGS: "You're tired of all this clutter."

POSITIVE INTENT: "You wish we'd keep this place a lot cleaner."

Practice 2. Larry says, "I'm so fed up with that job!" A block to expressing feelings might be giving advice: "Why don't you just quit?" Other responses might help him explore how he feels and what he'd like to do.

PARAPHRASE: "That job's been such a hassle."

REFLECTING FEELINGS: "You sound really demoralized."

POSITIVE INTENT: "You wish you had a job you could really connect with."

Now try listening to each other about some of your own issues. Speak for yourself, about your own *feelings* (see chapter 3, "Expressing Feelings")—don't take this opportunity to analyze or interpret your partner. When you listen to your partner's feelings, they eventually change. He may just want you to understand how he feels, or he could have a problem that needs a solution; either way, all you need to do in the beginning is listen.

Attention, paraphrasing, reflecting feelings, and recognizing positive intent will help you empathize with your partner. Despite learning these skills, there may be times when you end up in an argument in which neither of you feels heard. Having a quarrel is a sign that you're too upset or defensive to listen. Rather than withdrawing and avoiding the conflict, you can come back again later when you've cooled off, and try listening to each other then.

Questions and Comments

Q: Are you really suggesting we reflect everything someone says?

A: Most of the time you can just pay attention, and then respond with your own thoughts or feelings. Paraphrasing and reflecting feelings help you acknowledge your partner, so he can listen to you. You can use these skills to slow your interaction when you're both upset, so the conflict is less likely to escalate.

Q: If my partner's upset because he doesn't know what really happened, why not just explain it? Why reflect feelings when there's no reason for him to be upset?

A: If it works, fine; but sometimes it's difficult for someone to take in new information when he's angry or hurt. If he gets more upset when you try to explain yourself, back off and listen to him first, rather than interrupting him with your explanation.

Q: Why avoid arguments? Isn't that how we get to the bottom of how we really feel?

A: These skills aren't meant to avoid conflict, but to help you clarify what your conflict is really about. During a quarrel you may voice resentments that wouldn't have come up otherwise. You can make good use of your argument by discussing these issues once you've cooled off. Then they're less likely to build to the point where you need another blowup to talk about them.

3

Expressing Feelings

Men are socialized not to express emotional vulnerability, and we tend to rationalize our feelings by telling ourselves there's no reason to feel sad, hurt, or insecure. But an intimate relationship is based on feelings, so you're more likely to resolve conflicts with your partner when you take your emotions into account.

We've seen how listening can help you identify deeper feelings and keep conflict from escalating. In this chapter we'll look at how to get in touch with your own feelings and express them in a way that's likely to elicit a cooperative response from your partner.

Ten Ways to Think About Feelings

Feelings are slippery things. To our logical minds, they seem contradictory and confusing. Though they don't operate rationally, we can use what we know about feelings to express ourselves more effectively:

1. You don't have to justify feelings.
2. Feelings press for acknowledgment.
3. Feelings often shift once they're acknowledged.
4. Unacknowledged feelings tend to be acted out.
5. What you do is sometimes an indication of how you feel.
6. Being aware of a feeling doesn't mean you have to act on it.

7. Unacknowledged feelings may cause psychological and physical symptoms.
8. Anger often masks hurt, sadness, or fear.
9. Feelings may be clues to underlying issues in our relationships.
10. Expressing feelings enhances intimacy.

Let's go through this list to see how understanding feelings can help you gain more confidence in handling your emotions.

1. You Don't Have to Justify Feelings
Feelings simply exist; there is no right or wrong in how we feel. We may wish we felt differently, but we don't have to justify our feelings in order to feel them. We feel what we feel, sometimes regardless of whatever the "facts" may be. Though we may be able to sort out why we feel a certain way, in the beginning we can just be aware of how we feel.

2. Feelings Press for Acknowledgment
Feelings "want" to be recognized, and they continue to push into our awareness until we acknowledge them. They may come to us in dreams, or express themselves through moods, fantasies, and behavior.

3. Feelings Often Shift Once They're Acknowledged
Feelings are transitory. Sometimes just being aware of your feelings is enough for them to change. They may also shift when your partner empathizes with you. Knowing that feelings aren't permanent allows you more freedom to explore your emotions.

4. Unacknowledged Feelings Tend to Be Acted Out
When we push feelings away, they still manage to express themselves. You're likely to displace feelings you're not aware of by getting angry in traffic, kicking the dog, or yelling at your lover. The less aware we are of our feelings, the more likely we are to act them out.

5. What You Do is Sometimes an Indication of How You Feel
Since we tend to act out whatever we don't allow ourselves to feel, looking at our behavior can tell us a lot about our feelings.

If you find yourself being combative or defensive with your partner, maybe you're angry—perhaps at him, or maybe at yourself. As you pay more attention to how you feel, your emotions shift, or deepen. You become more aware of what you're really upset about as other feelings emerge—perhaps you feel neglected or hurt, you're frustrated that you're not living up to your potential, or you feel sad about a loss or disappointment.

6. Being Aware of a Feeling Doesn't Mean You Have to Act on It

We make decisions based partly on what we know and partly on how we feel. Just because you're aware of your feelings doesn't mean you have to act in a certain way or express them inappropriately. Your judgment and control don't disappear just because you realize how hurt or sad you are. Since unacknowledged feelings aren't pressing for expression, you actually have *more* control when you know how you feel. Then you can use your intelligence, experience, and imagination to figure out what you want to do.

7. Unacknowledged Feelings May Cause Psychological and Physical Symptoms

Unacknowledged feelings can be the real source of depression, anxiety, and boredom. They can also lead to physical symptoms, such as tension headaches, backaches, digestive problems, and ulcers.

8. Anger Often Masks Hurt, Sadness, or Fear

Because it's more acceptable for men to be in touch with anger, we may overlook the hurt, sadness, or fear that's underneath the anger. When we can identify the underlying feelings of sadness or hurt, it's often a lot easier for our partner to listen to us.

We may also have more than one feeling at once, which can be confusing. Just because we feel angry, for example, doesn't mean we can't also feel loving or sad as well.

9. Feelings May Be Clues to Underlying Issues in Our Relationships

Sometimes we're not aware of exactly what we're upset about. Though feelings are nonrational, they usually make sense. You may be jealous, for example, even if your partner is not interested in anyone else. But instead of putting yourself down for being irrational or paranoid, you can explore whether this feeling is a clue to some other issue. Discovering that you're sensitive about his attention toward others may help you realize you'd like more attention yourself.

10. Expressing Feelings Enhances Intimacy

Intimacy derives from our willingness to disclose our hopes and desires, especially toward each other. You may not always be very clear about what you feel or why. Having a responsive partner who listens and reflects can deepen your awareness of your emotions and help you feel more confident in expressing how you really feel.

Feelings versus Interpretations

People often confuse feelings with what are really interpretations of each other's behavior. When you're in touch with how you feel, you can communicate your feelings without blaming or interpreting your partner.

Starting with "I feel" doesn't necessarily mean you're saying anything about your emotions. In common speech, we've learned to say "I feel—" but then proceed to offer interpretations or judgments: "I feel you're being unreasonable," or "I feel like you're not really trying."

Whenever you say "I feel you—" or "I feel like—," you're probably interpreting or judging your partner, rather than disclosing how you feel. While an interpretation may be an attempt to make sense of his behavior, it tends to elicit a defensive response.

Behind most interpretations is something you want or something you fear. When you're in touch with the desire or fear, you can reveal something about yourself; then you're less likely to get into an argument over your interpretation. For example, the statement "You're so aloof" implies that you would like to feel closer, and you wonder whether your partner wants to feel closer too. So rather than accuse him of being aloof, you could say "I'd like to be closer to you." You're revealing something about yourself, rather than interpreting or judging him. Instead of arguing about whether he's aloof, he may be open to exploring what you could do together that would help you feel closer.

Similarly, you could state your concern in terms of your fears—"I wonder whether you're really interested in me." Rather than telling him he's aloof, you're asking for feedback. Then he can tell you how he feels toward you, without becoming defensive. By disclosing how you feel and what you want, you're more likely to elicit a cooperative response than if you interpret each other's behavior.

Conflict Styles

We often end up in conflict before we really know how we feel. A style of handling problems that acknowledges feelings is more likely to lead to successful conflict resolution. There are four main styles of dealing with irritations in a relationship: passive; aggressive; passive-aggressive; and assertive.

Passive

A passive response tries to ignore the conflict. You hope he'll get the hint or somehow figure out what you want without your having to say anything. But simply hoping that the problem will go away doesn't address what you're upset about.

Aggressive

A hostile response to a trangression lets the other person know you don't like his behavior by putting him down or threatening him. It's obvious that you're upset, but a counterattack tends to escalate the conflict.

Passive-aggressive

A passive-aggressive response is likely when you don't say what's upsetting you but still feel resentful. Your anger comes out in other ways, such as snide remarks, a cold shoulder, not following through on agreements, or the "silent treatment."

Assertive

An assertive response identifies the offending behavior and states how you feel about it. When you express yourself assertively, you're less likely to be passive-aggressive or to escalate the conflict through a counterattack.

The first three styles of handling (or avoiding) conflict are very common. We give someone the silent treatment, expecting him to know what we're upset about. Or we ignore irritations until we're fed up and can't stand it anymore, then pull out all the stops for a knock-down, drag-out fight. Of course you feel irritated by shabby treatment, but an assertive response is more likely to elicit cooperation from your partner than if you let things build up and then behave passive-aggressively or explode in anger.

The Assertive Response

Let's look at the following example to illustrate an assertive expression of feelings:

You're out on the street and your lover turns around to look at another man as he passes by. If it bothers you, to say nothing would be a passive response. To tell him off right on the street would be aggressive. And to give him the cold shoulder later, making him beg you to tell him what's wrong, would be passive-aggressive. An assertive message would identify his behavior and say how you felt about it.

Behavior and feelings are the basic elements of an assertive message. Let's look at each of these elements and see how we can use them to approach the above conflict.

Behavior

When you're upset with your partner, it's usually because of something he did (or neglected to do). By identifying the actual behavior (what he did or didn't *do*) you're more likely to disclose how it affects you rather than interpret his motives. In the above example, what's the behavior? He "turned around to look at another man." To say he "ogled" or "cruised" the other man would be an *interpretation* of his behavior.

Feelings

The part of the message that involves the most self-disclosure is how you feel about his behavior. If you accuse him of cruising, your feelings get lost in an argument over your interpretation, rather than letting him know how you felt about him looking at another man.

Ask yourself how you feel: "I feel insecure" or "I feel jealous." He's less likely to get defensive when you say how you feel, rather than interpreting his behavior.

Let's put the behavior and feelings together to see what an assertive response might look like: (1) the behavior or event ("looking at another man") and (2) how you feel about it ("insecure").

Instead of saying "It really bugs me when you cruise other guys," which could easily lead to an argument about whether he was cruising, you could say "When you look at other guys, I feel insecure."

Perhaps he recognized someone, or maybe he was just "enjoying the scenery." In any case, he'll be more willing to consider how you feel in response to his behavior if he doesn't feel compelled to defend himself against a negative interpretation.

Effects

A third component of an assertive message is how the behavior affects you. In the above example, the only effect was how you felt about it. But sometimes there may be tangible effects to your partner's behavior that you can identify, which will clarify why you're upset. For example, if he leaves dishes in the sink, the tangible effect is that you have to clean up before you can make dinner.

Solutions

It can be tempting to add a fourth part to an assertive message: offering a solution. Often this is implied by what you're upset about. If you're feeling comfortable with each other, there's nothing wrong with simply saying what you want: "I wish you'd clean up after yourself" or "Could you turn down the stereo?"

But when you're upset with each other, saying what you want before you've both said how you feel can lead to a debate over possible solutions. It may be more useful to explore how you feel about it first.

Once you've had a chance to express your feelings, you may feel differently about how you'd like the behavior to change. In the former example, if your boyfriend is able to reassure you about his caring for you, maybe you'll both enjoy looking at other guys on the street. What you're willing to consider as a possible solution to a problem may shift as you explore how you feel.

Assertiveness Exercises

As with the listening exercises, it's useful to practice with neutral material. The purpose of these exercises is to build your skill in communicating clearly. Attempting to solve every conflict in your relationship is not realistic when you're first starting out. Use the following examples to practice, and then identify behaviors and feelings about issues that exist in your own relationship.

Exercise 1. Your partner arrives an hour late, without calling.

BEHAVIOR: Coming home late without calling.
FEELING: Annoyed and worried.
EFFECT: You're late for the concert.

A blameful message might be: "I 'feel' you were really inconsiderate for not calling."

An assertive message identifies the behavior, describes how it affects you, and lets your partner know how you feel about it. Putting this all together might look something like this: "I was worried when you didn't call. And I feel annoyed that we're going to be late for the concert."

This example includes all the elements; but of course people don't usually talk this way. In an actual relationship, you would already know the context, so you wouldn't need to spell it out. Your tone of voice would also indicate that you feel annoyed. Instead of the entire statement noted above, you might pick one part of the message to emphasize: "We're going to be late" or "I wish you had called."

Your partner will recognize that you're annoyed; there's probably no need for him to say "You must be upset I didn't call." But he might acknowledge you by saying "Sorry I didn't call."

Exercise 2. He leaves the gas tank empty, and you're late for work.

BEHAVIOR: Not filling up the tank.
FEELING: Angry.
EFFECT: You're late for work.

An interpretation might be: "I 'feel' you don't really care about me."

An assertive message (citing the behavior and its effect): "You left the tank empty, and I was late to work."

A reflective reply: "I bet you were mad."

Exercise 3. You agreed to alternate chores, and he forgets to take out the trash.

BEHAVIOR: The trash wasn't taken out.
FEELING: Irritated.
EFFECT: The can is full for another week.

An interpretation: "I 'feel' you're not really trying."

An assertive message (with just the behavior): "The trash wasn't taken out."

A reflective reply: "You must be annoyed I keep forgetting."

Listening Is the Primary Skill

People often hesitate to tell someone what they're upset about for fear the other person will become so defensive that nobody will get heard. In the past, you may have suffered from your parents' rages, had difficulties with uncontrolled outbursts, or been rejected for being extremely upset. Since a lot of damage can result from the unbridled expression of negative feelings, you may have concluded that emotional expression is actually dangerous for a relationship. Yet it's possible to express anger without being concerned that you will physically harm someone, and you can be upset without becoming "hysterical" or "losing it." It's not that easy, but being more in touch with your feelings will help you develop your ability to handle conflict.

In many ways, listening is the primary skill. Even if you say how you feel with a nonaccusatory, assertive message, your partner may still become defensive. You can step back for a moment and reflect his feelings until he feels calm enough to listen to you. You can both contribute to de-escalating a conflict by admitting that you feel defensive and by listening to your partner.

Questions and Comments

Q: My lover won't tell me what's wrong when he's upset, so I end up provoking a fight just to get a reaction out of him.

A: It sounds as if you're caught in a vicious circle: your attempt to elicit feelings is met by withdrawal, and his withdrawal stimulates you to provoke a fight. He thinks you're being intrusive, and you experience him as withholding.

Acknowledge your difference in how you deal with feelings, and discuss your impulse to provoke him in order to get a reaction. He may be just as dissatisfied with this dynamic as you are; perhaps he'd be willing to explore another way to handle your different styles.

Q: My boyfriend is really manipulative. If he doesn't get what he wants, he pouts and sulks until I give in.

A: Accusing someone of being manipulative usually elicits a defensive response. "Pouting" and "sulking" are also loaded terms. You can identify his behavior with a more neutral description and say how you feel about it, instead of giving in.

BEHAVIOR: He claims you never want to do anything with him, and then withdraws.

FEELING: You feel annoyed.

You can also reflect his feelings: "It sounds as if you feel neglected." Then you can explore how you could spend time together so he doesn't feel rejected and you don't feel imposed upon.

Q: Once I admitted to my lover I have some fears about intimacy. Now every time we have an argument he throws it in my face, claiming my fear of intimacy is the real issue, no matter what we're arguing about.

A: As mentioned earlier, interpretations tend to elicit a defensive response. You end up arguing about whether you have a character defect, instead of dealing with the desire or fear behind his interpretation: what does he want from you, or what is he afraid of? Then you can say how you feel, too. Rather than arguing about his interpretation, you can negotiate for what you want.

Q: My boyfriend said I'm really immature. When I objected, he said "I'm just being honest about my feelings."

A: "Immature" is a judgement, not a feeling. If he can identify the *behavior* that irritates him, you can work on solving the problem, instead of arguing about whether you're immature.

4

Solving Problems

*E*ncountering problems in a relationship can be unsettling. The impulse to offer solutions or defend ourselves arises from our anxiety in dealing with emotions. But trying to solve the problem right away can interfere with the expression of feelings. Exploring how we feel helps us clarify the desires we'd like a potential solution to address. When we feel understood, we're likely to consider a greater range of possible solutions.

In a moment we'll present a systematic method for resolving conflicts. But before we get into solving problems, let's summarize some of the points we've made in previous discussions about listening and expressing feelings.

Ten-Point Guide for Approaching Conflict

1. Listen without interrupting.

2. Reflect what you've understood before giving your side of the conflict.

3. Imagine how you would feel if you had your partner's perception of the current problem.

4. Identify the behavior's that bother you and how you feel about them.

5. Say how you feel, rather than interpreting or analyzing your partner.

6. Avoid sarcasm and blame.

7. Don't use sensitive issues to put each other down.

8. Use your partner's defensiveness as a signal to back off and listen.

9. Acknowledge your own defensiveness, so your partner can listen to you.

10. Give your partner the benefit of the doubt—listen for positive intent.

Remember that if you're so upset your conflict escalates into a quarrel, you can always come back to listen to each other once you've cooled off.

Agreements

It helps to have an understanding about how, when, and where you'll bring up issues that bother you. You may decide not to have discussions about your sex life or finances in front of friends, for example; or there may be some places that feel safer for you to work out disagreements—at home rather than in public, perhaps; in or out of bed, and so on.

Say how you feel about yelling, swearing, and moving around dramatically. Some people really enjoy letting go. For others, yelling was a sign while growing up that conflicts were about to escalate out of control, and it's frightening. You can work out a style that feels comfortable and natural, and let each other know when you want to slow things down.

Remember that taking a break can also help you sort through your feelings and keep conflicts from escalating. You can agree beforehand on how to call time out and how long it will last, so it's not experienced as an unfair abandonment of the dispute.

Timing

Even if your partner approaches you with an assertive, nonaccusatory message, you may not always be in the mood to listen to his concerns as soon as you walk through the door. When you come home from work, you may want to unwind or be by yourself for a while. You may prefer to have dinner be a time when you talk about how your day went, what's new, or what you're looking forward to. When you go to bed, negotiating chores may be the last thing you're interested in. Over the course of a week, there may be few occasions when issues you need to deal with arise spontaneously.

Rather than let things slide, some couples set aside a time when they both know they'll be giving their full attention to what's bothering them. You won't feel so pressured to discuss something just as your partner is leaving for work if you know that you'll be getting together later.

It's important not to overload your discussion with so many issues that it becomes aversive; otherwise you'll avoid meeting. Don't simply dwell on problems—tell each other what you appreciate about each other, as well.

Do something fun together afterward, as a positive reinforcement for sticking through difficult issues. Of course, there may be occasions when you'll prefer to be by yourself after a particularly intense negotiation. Other ideas related to your earlier discussion may occur to you, but be careful not to process your relationship to death.[1] You need some time just to be with and enjoy each other.

Focusing

When you get together to work through problems, make a list of the issues you want to discuss. Set some priorities—each of you can choose one topic that stands out for you the most. One conflict may remind you of other resentments, but it's more productive to address one issue at a time.

What first draws your attention may be an example of a larger problem that bothers you—the bread crumbs left on the counter may remind you that you're tired of cleaning up after your partner all over the house. But instead of using various examples to prove he's a "slob," you can broaden the specific incident to a discussion of cleanliness expectations.

If other issues arise, you can agree to come back to them later, or negotiate a shift. Don't jump to "how many checks you bounced last month" when you're planning your vacation or dividing up chores. Instead, add it to the list and go back to what you were working on. When you reach an agreement, write it down. This will help clarify your thoughts and serve as a common memory you can return to later.

Successful resolution of one conflict may encourage you to tackle other problems, but you probably won't resolve everything in one meeting. Appreciate each other for your efforts, and set aside discussion of the other issues until the next time you get together.

Six-Step Program for Resolving Conflicts

It's useful to divide problem-solving into a number of steps. Following this outline can help you sort through your feelings and desires, stay focused on the issue at hand, and ensure that you'll both get a chance to express yourselves. This makes it a lot easier to listen without interrupting.

Step 1. Clarify the conflict.
    1a. Say what you'd like.
    1b. Distinguish desires from potential solutions.
    1c. Identify behaviors and feelings; listen and reflect.

Step 2. Brainstorm alternatives.

Step 3. Examine potential solutions to see if they meet both your desires. If none do:
    3a. Take a break.
    3b. Shift from the content of the conflict to valuing the relationship.
    3c. Think about what you could offer to resolve the impasse.
    3d. Come back and say what you're willing to offer.
    3e. Return to brainstorming.

Step 4. Select a tentative solution.

Step 5. Try out the solution for a trial run.

Step 6. Set aside time to evaluate how it's working.

To illustrate how these steps work with an actual conflict, we'll use the following situation as an example:

Jess and Frank have been living together in Seattle for a few years. Frank has been accepted for graduate school at the University of Washington, and also at Boston University. He's from Boston originally, and he thinks Boston's program would be better for his purposes than Washington's. Jess has lived in Seattle for years—his friends are in the Northwest, he has a career that's going well, and he has no desire to move. Let's look at how Frank and Jess use these steps to figure out how to deal with their conflicting desires.

Step 1. Clarify the Conflict

1a. Say what you'd like. It's easier to stay focused on a particular issue when you're able to identify what the conflict is about. This may seem obvious, but it's easy to get sidetracked when you're upset with each other. We'll be going into how the problem affects you and how you feel about it in a moment. In the beginning, each partner says what he'd like, without trying to justify it.

FRANK: I'd like to go to Boston for graduate school, and I'd like you to come with me.

JESS: I'd rather stay in Seattle, so why don't you go to the University of Washington?

1b. Distinguish desires from potential solutions. The goal of conflict resolution is to find a solution that meets both your desires. An argument over the first solution that comes to mind can distract you from exploring other options that might be able to satisfy you. Identifying your desires can help you clarify the problem you hope a potential solution will resolve.

"Moving to Boston" is a possible solution. Frank says what he hopes to achieve by going to Boston: "I'd like to get the best education possible." This is the desire behind the potential solution of moving to Boston.

For Jess, "staying in Seattle" is also a solution. What's his desire? "To further my career."

Following is a list of their potential solutions, matched with their underlying desires.

Potential solutions	Underlying desires
Moving to Boston	Best education
Staying in Seattle	Further career

Instead of getting into a debate over "moving to Boston versus staying in Seattle," they shift the focus of their efforts to figuring out a way for Frank to get the best education and for Jess to further his career. These are the real desires behind the possible solution of either moving or staying. They may still have to decide between the two cities, but this shift can help them explore solutions that will take both their desires into account.

1c. *Identify behaviors and feelings; listen and reflect.* In this example, the behavior in question might be identified as Frank's plans to pursue his education at Boston University. In the following exchange, Jess and Frank discuss and reflect how this would affect each of them.

JESS: If I came along, I'd feel resentful about losing my job and leaving my friends. But if I stayed behind, I'm not sure our relationship would last.

FRANK: You want to keep your job and your friends, but you wonder whether our relationship would survive if I left without you. [He listens to Jess and reflects his concerns, then continues.] I'd miss you if you didn't come with me. If I stayed in Seattle, I might be able to make the best of this program, but I'd also feel resentful. I feel really torn.

JESS: You'd rather go to Boston, but you feel torn between our relationship and your career. [He listens and reflects.]

They both acknowledge that they would like to keep living together. Behind the solution of "living together" is the desire to maintain their relationship. So they add this to the underlying desires they listed above:

Underlying desires

Best education
Further career
Maintain relationship

This is really the crux of their conflict—if it weren't for their desire to maintain their relationship, Frank could move to Boston and Jess could wish him well. This may seem obvious, but when you're faced with a conflict it helps to acknowledge your caring for each other. This helps you remember why you're struggling so hard to work something out.

At this point the conflict is fairly clear, in terms of both how they would each be affected by moving or staying and how they feel about it. They've also identified the basic desires that each would like met by a potential solution. Now they're ready to move on to the next step.

Step 2. Brainstorm Alternatives

Brainstorming is a process of generating a lot of possibilities very quickly, without editing or evaluating. It was developed for creative problem-solving in various work settings. Brainstorming taps into the more imaginative and playful parts of our minds for creative solutions. One of its main advantages is that it keeps us from getting stuck in a debate over the first solution that comes to mind. In our example with Jess and Frank, they could easily get sidetracked over whether Boston is more culturally stimulating than Seattle. Instead, brainstorming can help them come up with a creative solution to their underlying desires.

Brainstorming works like this: you ask yourselves "What are possible solutions that could meet both our desires?" Then very quickly, without evaluating, you call them out and write them down on a list. No editing! Give free reign to your imagination. Usually some suggestions are so outrageous you can't help but laugh. A playful approach to problem-solving helps you consider a wider range of possibilities.

Don't evaluate every suggestion; just write it down and plunge ahead. The whole point of brainstorming is to put off evaluating until you've thoroughly mined the resources of your creative imagination, which tends to shy away from the harsh light of evaluation. Save that step until later.

Frank and Jess come up with the following list:

Both move to Boston, and Jess could start his own business.
Stay in Seattle.
Frank could go to Boston, but come back for breaks.
Jess could visit Boston during breaks.
Frank could visit Boston and talk to people to see if Boston's program really lives up to its reputation.
Jess could ask at work about a transfer to Boston.
Frank could talk to people in his field at the University of Washington.
Move Jess's friends to Boston.

Frank could go to Boston for the first year, then do his fieldwork in Seattle.

Jess could support Frank if he stayed in Seattle.

Forget school and work—let's go to Thailand!

Step 3. Examine Potential Solutions to See If They Meet Both Your Desires

Go over the brainstorming list to see how each suggestion would work for you. Reflecting how you both feel about these options will provide you with some confidence that your needs will be addressed.

Frank is willing to question his assumption that Boston has a better program, and Jess is willing to see if he could transfer to Boston. They decide to pursue these ideas and put off further problem-solving until they have more information. Frank talks to students in Seattle, then flies to Boston to interview recent graduates and professors. Jess asks at work about a transfer. The following week they get back together.

FRANK: Either school would prepare me for a career, but Boston's program sounds a lot more interesting. What did you find out?

JESS: They're closing our office in Boston, so there's no way I could transfer. [They look at some of the other options on their list.] What about doing your second-year field placement in Seattle?

FRANK: That can't be arranged until the end of the first year.

JESS [pausing for a moment]: What if you stayed here, and I supported you?

FRANK: Be serious. I threw that in as a joke.

JESS: No, really. We could get by if you got some loans to cover tuition. Going to Boston, you'll be in debt forever.

FRANK: I'm not sure I'd feel comfortable having you support me.

JESS: Well, think about it. I'm not trying to buy you off, but I'd be willing to help out.

Step 4. Select a Tentative Solution

By the time you reach this step, you may have narrowed it down to a few options, each of which has its good points and drawbacks. Sometimes a combination of possibilities from your brainstorming list will emerge as the best solution, or another idea will occur to you. What seemed like a bottom line when you first began this process may shift as you gradually discover what's really important to you.

Empathizing with each other's position can help you stay flexible in what you're willing to consider, even with difficult problems. Not that you have to tiptoe through every interaction; when a certain level of trust is established, it's likely you can sail through much of this. But you have some tools for sorting through your feelings if the process bogs down.

In the above example, Frank decides to take Jess up on his offer to support him while he's in school, and they work out some clear expectations about how much Frank will be expected to contribute.

Step 5. Try Out the Solution for a Trial Run
You define what each of you will do and try it out. One way you can make the choice seem less imposing is to see it as an experiment: give it a chance to work for a specified period of time, then evaluate how it's working.

Make the trial long enough to give it a fair chance, but short enough so that neither of you feels overly burdened by a solution that's not meeting your needs. You don't have to talk about it every time you see each other. Rather than using the first snag to justify why it won't work, see what you can do to make it work.

If you're negotiating a new system for chores, you'll be able to see how it's working within a few days or weeks. In the situation above, Frank and Jess decide they'll have to see how school goes for at least the first semester.

Step 6. Set Aside Time to Evaluate How It's Working
Did this solution take care of the desires you identified previously? When you put your solution into practice, you may get in touch with other desires, or think of another way to address the problem. Take turns listening to each other, and reflect what you've understood.

After the first semester, Frank is dissatisfied with his program. He may want to negotiate a transfer to Boston for the second year; or perhaps he realizes that every graduate program has its good and bad points and he can make the best of it. Or they look at Jess's ability to support both of them on half of what they used to earn, and decide they'd like Frank to work part time after all.

Impasse

What if your brainstorming list fails to generate solutions that satisfy your desires? Rather than assuming your differences are insurmountable, you can take a break in order to get some perspective on the importance of this conflict in your relationship.

Let's say that in the above example Frank comes back from his trip convinced that Boston has a better program. Meanwhile, Jess finds out they're cutting back his hours at work, so he couldn't support both of them even if he wanted to. They look at the rest of their list, and though they could settle for flying back and forth across the country, they feel discouraged. They recognize they're at an impasse, and go on to the second part of Step 3:

Step 3. Examine potential solutions to see if they meet both your desires. If none do:
   3a. Take a break.
   3b. Shift from the content of the conflict to valuing the relationship.
   3c. Think about what you could offer to resolve the impasse.
   3d. Come back and say what you're willing to offer.
   3e. Return to brainstorming.

3a. Take a break. You don't have to turn these sessions into marathons. When you reach an impasse, you might as well take a break and set a time to get back together. Jess and Frank agree to meet again in two days.

3b. Shift from the content of the conflict to valuing the relationship. How important is this problem? On their own, they shift from the content of this particular conflict to the value of their relationship. Staying together as a couple may be considerably more important to both of them than living in Seattle or moving to Boston.

*3c. **Think about what you could offer to resolve the impasse.*** In the midst of an argument, we tend to polarize. Once you've gotten some distance, it's easier to consider how you might contribute to a solution. Your willingness to try something new may influence your partner to cooperate as well.

*3d. **Come back and say what you're willing to offer.*** Frank and Jess both realize that staying together is worth some trade-offs on their other desires.

JESS: I was thinking, if they're cutting back my hours, why should I be that committed to staying in Seattle anyway?

FRANK: I'd miss you an awful lot, and was thinking I could at least come back during breaks. I could also press for a commitment about doing my second-year fieldwork in Seattle.

They come to the following agreement: Jess will request a year's leave of absence, and Frank will ask for a commitment from Boston for a second-year placement in Seattle. Since this solution is dependent on outside decisions, they come up with contingency plans in case either of their requests is turned down. Jess may decide to quit his job anyway, or Frank will go to the University of Washington if he can't get that commitment from Boston. Remembering the last suggestion on their brainstorming list ("Forget school and work—let's go to Thailand!"), they decide to take a trip before Frank dives into graduate school.

What If There Are Still Problems?

You may not find the best solution the first time around. Sometimes you don't really know how you'll react until you've given it a trial run. You may discover underlying desires you weren't aware of before, or other ideas occur to you that might work better.

Though it may feel frustrating to go through this process again, it's helpful to remember that we often have to practice other skills, without being perfect the first time through. Mistakes are simply a form of feedback: when you miss a key on the piano, you learn how far to extend your fingers; when you take a spill on the ski slope, you discover when to pull out of a turn. Likewise, when dealing with conflicts, you learn when to say what you want and when to back off and listen; you try out a solution and find out whether it really works for you.

Now, it may be that your conflicting desires really are stronger than the bond that holds your relationship together. You may feel saddened by this loss, but you can feel confident that you've explored various options. You're less likely to split up prematurely, with regrets about not having at least tried to figure out what else you could have done.

In the above example, what if part of the reason Frank wanted to go to Boston was because he felt ambivalent about the relationship? Then it would be better to talk about his uncertainty with Jess. Though graduate school might still be a major decision for Frank, having a dispute over moving to Boston might be a sidetrack from what's really bothering him. If they stay with this process, he might become aware of his ambivalence when they reach an impasse. Then they could deal with the real issue, rather than splitting up because he "had to" move to Boston, without ever expressing his true feelings.

You may not be aware of your feelings when you first start out. That's all right; clarifying how you feel is what this process is for. An authentic exchange depends on your willingness to say how you feel, empathize with your partner, and negotiates a solution that satisfies both of you. In the process of solving problems, you find out more about yourself and you get to know each other better. Other decisions sometimes fall into place once you've clarified your desire to stay together. As you work through major issues, you reach a new level of commitment to your relationship.

Exercise

Take some issue, such as dividing chores, that's not the most crucial conflict in your relationship. Go through the steps for resolving conflicts and talk about your cleanliness expectations. Say how you'd keep things if you lived by yourself. Identify areas in which you have different priorities—for example, you might like a clean kitchen but not pay much attention to clothes being left around the living room, while your partner can't stand clutter but rarely notices dust.

Brainstorm and see what options you come up with—you may end up rotating chores, specializing in chores that you each care about more, or hiring a cleaning person to help you out. Go through the steps until you've reached an agreement; then try it out for a couple of weeks.

Come back and say how it worked. If you didn't follow through, explore how you felt. Did taking out the trash remind you of being yelled at as a kid? Do you hate cleaning the bathroom? Did you hold back when discussing what you really want in terms of cleanliness standards? Did you give in to please your partner, without realizing how you'd feel about doing your chore? If you were both too busy, what does that say about your priorities? To ensure that you'll follow through, you need to be honest about what you want; otherwise, you'll sabotage your agreements.

When trying something new, it's heartening to have your attempts at change recognized and appreciated, even if you haven't reached the goals you set for yourselves. Notice your partner's efforts; in addition to identifying problem areas, tell each other what you liked about what you've each contributed toward making things work.

We've looked at the importance of identifying underlying desires, so you're less likely to get into a debate over the first solution that comes to mind. When feelings are heard and accepted, they often shift, which can alter how you perceive the conflict. Using the steps outlined above can give you a structure for resolving conflicts that recognize feelings, values the relationship, and facilitates solutions that take the needs and desires of both partners into account.

Questions and Comments

Q: My lover and I have tried these steps, but it rarely goes that smoothly.

A: The examples in this book are condensed and simplified in order to give you an idea of the range of options available for working through conflicts. In real life, two lovers might not be quite so elaborate in their feedback, nor be able to say how they feel right away. Most of us muddle through, mixing feelings and judgments, interpreting each other, arguing about solutions, and not listening extremely closely. When you get stuck, you can use these methods to extricate yourselves from interactions that aren't working the way you'd like.

Q: How can I use these steps when my boyfriend is so stubborn he refuses to negotiate?

A: Everyone feels exasperated with his partner at times, but there's not much to be gained by trying to convince him he's being stubborn. Instead, see his resistance as a signal for you to listen. Try to understand what's at stake for him—perhaps he feels he has already given up too much in the past. When you understand the source of his resistance, deeper feelings will emerge and it will become clearer what your conflict is really about.

5

The Function of Conflict

Problems in a relationship can often be solved by using the steps we outlined in the previous chapter—you clarify the problem and work out a solution that satisfies your underlying desires. But sometimes a simple conflict mushrooms into a competitive struggle, and you realize it carries a significance beyond its obvious content.

A relationship is a system of mutual influence: each person's behavior influences (and is influenced by) his partner. Understanding this influence, we're less likely to assume that either partner is "bad" or "crazy" for reacting in a certain way. Our feelings and behavior usually make sense in the context of our relationships. Rather than seeing conflict as a threat and avoiding it, we can use our problems to identify and change unsatisfying patterns.

Unspoken Accommodations

A major source of problems in relationships is our tendency to accommodate each other without negotiating our desires. Obviously we need to meet our partners halfway at times in order to even have a relationship. But there's a danger in making too many compromises without saying what you want or checking out your assumptions. You may not realize how much you've given up until you feel resentful, stubborn, or unwilling to cooperate in a seemingly minor dispute.

In the following example with Mike and Al, we'll see how a conflict over watching television during dinner escalates, leaving them confused and mistrustful. By identifying their unspoken accommodations, they discover how they each contributed to the negative cycle that developed between them. We'll use their conflict to show how you can interrupt similar patterns in your own relationship.

Mike is in the kitchen when Al comes home. Al calls out, "Hi! Smells great!" and stashes his briefcase in the den. While he washes up, Mike puts dinner on the table. Al joins him in the kitchen and turns on the television.

Mike sits down and says, "How was your day?"

Al says, "All right." He watches the news while serving himself.

Mike takes a bite, then puts down his fork. "Couldn't we have dinner without the news for a change?"

Al looks over and says, "What?"

MIKE: Couldn't we have a conversation?
AL: Sure. What's happening?
MIKE: I mean without the TV.
AL: I want to watch the news.
MIKE: I find it a little distracting.
AL: Is something up?
MIKE: Not especially; I'd just like to talk.
AL: Well, so talk to me.
MIKE: I was trying to.
AL: Nothing much happened today. It was so-so. What about you? [Mike is explaining how his day went when there's an explosion on the screen.] Oh man, would you look at that! What a mess!
MIKE: That's exactly what I'm talking about.
AL: What?
MIKE: You weren't even listening to me; you're reacting to the TV.
AL: You said you got the class you wanted but you don't like the professor. [Al shovels in another mouthful.]

MIKE: All right, you heard what I said. But it's hard to talk with the TV on.

AL: I don't know—we could talk about the Middle East. What do you think of the latest peace initiative?

MIKE: Can we turn off the TV?

AL: What do you want to talk about?

MIKE: I just don't want to compete with the news.

AL: Well, if you don't have anything particular to say, do you mind if I watch my program?

Mike says, "Never mind." He gets up and takes his plate into the living room.

Back in the kitchen, Al bangs down his fork. He gets up and turns off the television. He stands in the doorway and says, "What's going on?"

MIKE: You'd obviously rather watch TV, so what does it matter?

AL: I turned it off, all right? Now what's wrong?

MIKE: If you can't figure it out, I'm not going to try to explain it to you.

"Well, then just piss off," Al says, disgusted, and returns to the kitchen. He dumps his dinner in the garbage and leaves the apartment, slamming the door behind him.

Discussion

A disagreement over watching TV while eating dinner has escalated to the point where they're furious with each other. What function does this conflict serve in their relationship? One way of figuring this out is by shifting from the *content* of their dispute to the *process* of what took place between them. The content was whether or not they should watch TV while eating dinner. The process was the power struggle that developed between them.

Al has just gotten home and would like some time to himself. Aside from keeping up with current events, watching the news helps him unwind after work. But dinner is ready, and he'd feel guilty if he told Mike he'd rather be by himself for a while. Because he silently accommodated Mike by not asking for some time alone, he feels irritated by Mike's request to turn off the TV; after he has already given in, Mike's request feels like an imposition. But Mike doesn't know that Al has accommodated him, so he thinks Al is being uncooperative and insensitive.

For Mike, eating dinner together is a way of affirming his sense of being a couple. He resents competing with the TV, but he doesn't say he wants attention; instead, he tries to *compel* Al's attention. His request to turn off the TV is an indirect expression of his desire for emotional closeness. But Al, who doesn't know that Mike is feeling neglected, experiences Mike's request as a power play.

For Al, watching TV becomes a means to express his independence. Then Mike withdraws to express his hurt, rather than saying how he feels. Al sees Mike as being manipulative, though he also understands that Mike is upset. He comes into the living room to acknowledge that they have a problem, yet he's obviously irritated with Mike's withdrawal. Feeling put down, Mike mistrusts Al's offer to listen and responds with sarcasm. This infuriates Al, who no longer wants to cooperate; instead of reflecting Mike's anger, he retaliates.

The stage was set for this dispute when Al discounted his desire for some time by himself. Then he accommodated Mike without stating his real preference. Because he still wanted to unwind, Al turned on the TV. At the same time, Mike wanted some attention. But instead of saying he wanted attention, Mike tried to compete with the TV, and their conflict escalated.

They both feel miserable over what seemed like a minor dispute, and neither partner really knows what hit him. Obviously something more is at stake than just the news, but they're unable to recognize their underlying problem, much less consider potential solutions that might address their desires. For Mike, the function of this conflict may be to affirm his importance to Al; and for Al, to assert his independence. Their views of each other's role in the conflict are mutually disconfirming: Mike sees Al as pushing him away, and Al sees Mike as clinging and trying to control him. In a moment we'll look at how they might extricate themselves from this difficulty. But first we'll consider what *seeing* each other as "clinging" and "pushing away" contributes to the pattern that has developed between them. To examine this possibility, let's look at the psychological defense called "projection."

Projection

Projection is the tendency to see in someone else a quality that we don't like about ourselves. Because we don't like it, we may see it *only* in others, and not realize it's something we do or feel ourselves.

For example, many of our stereotypes of other ethnic groups are related to projections, as are some cases of homophobia. The homophobic person may be unaware of his own same-sex attractions, and defend against these unacceptable feelings by projecting them onto gays, whom he sees as perverted, obsessed with sex, and so on. These are the judgments he would make about himself if he were to acknowledge his own homoerotic feelings. So, to protect his self-esteem, he can see "perversions" only in others.

Whenever we have a strong reaction to someone, it's useful to consider what that person reminds us of. Many of our opinions about others are judgments we would make about ourselves if we realized we had similar qualities. Reclaiming our projections can help us become more accepting of our own shortcomings, and less judgmental toward others.

Naturally, a close emotional relationship provides ample opportunity for projection. Al sees Mike as "clinging," not recognizing his own desire for closeness; and Mike sees Al as "aloof," ignoring his own desire for independence. When each partner complements disowned aspects of the other, they both contribute to a cycle known as "projective identification."[1]

Projective Identification

Projective identification occurs when we not only see a trait in our partner that we don't recognize in ourselves but also pressure him (in unconscious ways) to experience and act on our projection.[2]

In our example with Mike and Al, Mike may feel insecure about his own desire for separate activities. Doing things on his own may feel too risky, or it may seem contrary to his notions of intimacy. So he projects his desire for independence onto Al—he sees *Al* as being the one who wants distance in the relationship. In fact, he elicits distancing behavior in Al by making emotional demands when Al isn't likely to respond favorably. By doing so, he's able to experience some degree of independence, but he sees this desire as coming from Al. Meanwhile, he feels miserable because Al is so "aloof," and he remains oblivious to his own part in eliciting Al's rejecting behavior.

If Al didn't have any unresolved ambivalence about intimacy (and who of us doesn't?), he might be able to identify Mike's double message: Mike says he wants to be intimate, yet he pushes Al away. Commenting on this dynamic, Al would be less likely to play his part in the "script" that has developed between them, and Mike could get in touch with his own ambivalence about closeness and independence.

However, we often find partners who complement our own unconscious needs for projective identification, and they'll play right along with us. Al may feel anxious about being too close— so he projects his desire for closeness onto Mike. He sees Mike as the one who's "needy." But then Al elicits clinging behavior from Mike by not being emotionally available when Mike is obviously in pain. In this way, Al is able to experience feelings of closeness, but he sees this need as coming from Mike. He's tired of Mike's "clinging," but he doesn't see what he contributes to the cycle.

Mike could also comment on Al's double message: Al wants some time to himself, yet instead of saying so, he draws Mike into a competition for attention.

A move toward closeness by one partner may elicit a corresponding move toward distance by the other. Likewise, a move toward distance may elicit a desire to affirm closeness. Male couples often experience this dynamic shift back and forth, as the pursuer gives up and withdraws and his partner then pursues him.

If they could reclaim their desires for independence *and* closeness, they wouldn't need to project these needs onto each other. The goal is for each man to experience his own ambivalence about intimacy and independence without having to project one part of his ambivalence onto his partner. They would then be far less likely to elicit the very behavior they fear experiencing in themselves.

So how do we break out of a projective identification cycle? Part of the problem is that this process takes place outside of our conscious awareness. If you experience recurring conflicts that you seem unable to resolve, projective identification might be the problem.

Reclaiming Projections

You can use the following steps to identify and reclaim projections:

1. Consider the possibility that you may be projecting. What is it about your partner you don't like? Could this be a quality that you dislike about yourself?
2. How are emotional roles divided in your relationship? Is one of you "reasonable" while the other is "emotional"? One of you affectionate, while the other keeps to himself? Does one of you express your feelings, while the other is more reserved?
3. How might you be contributing to this division of labor? Is there anything you do that tends to elicit a complementary response from your partner?
4. Identify mixed messages you may be giving your partner— do you say you want to be close, yet your behavior pushes him away?
5. Identify the fears and desires behind your interpretations.
6. Talk about your expectations for emotional closeness and independent activity.

It's natural to feel ambivalent about intimacy and independence. You can recognize your ambivalence and experience this struggle within yourself, instead of projecting it onto your partner, compelling him to act out your disowned feelings. You'll be more likely to tolerate *his* ambivalence without seeing him as "clinging" or "rejecting" when your desires for closeness or separate activities clash.

Both partners contribute to the cycles that develop in a relationship. When you find yourselves caught in a negative pattern, consider what each of you is doing to elicit the very behavior you object to in your partner. We needn't see this process as pathological. It's inevitable that one partner will want some attention when the other wants time to himself. Sometimes this dynamic shifts simply by being recognized. Then you'll be able to negotiate whatever level of contact works for both of you.

Working Through the Underlying Conflict

How might Al and Mike use their awareness of these dynamics to resolve their conflict over watching TV during dinner? When Al returns home, they begin by acknowledging that they'd like to work something out. They listen to each other's hurt without trying to defend themselves. They reflect feelings and try to empathize with each other's experience. Feeling more comfortable with each other, they're able to acknowledge what each contributed to escalating the conflict.

AL: You obviously wanted to talk, so I can see how you felt rejected when I turned on the TV.

MIKE: Well, I'm sure my stomping off to the living room didn't help any. It must have seemed like an ultimatum.

They understand that Mike's attempt to express emotional closeness was experienced by Al as intrusive and controlling, and Al's desire for time to himself was experienced by Mike as rejecting. They begin to see this conflict as a signal that they've been accommodating each other without negotiating what they really want.

MIKE: When you brush me off, I wonder what's wrong.

AL: I always feel like I have to be doing something in order to justify being by myself. Just because I want to be alone for a while doesn't mean anything's wrong, or that I'm rejecting you.

MIKE: If you'd just tell me you'd rather be by yourself, I could handle that.

AL: And if you'd tell me you want some attention, then I'd feel more responsive. Or at least willing to negotiate.

Mike can ask for attention without compelling a choice between himself and Al's other interests. Similarly, Al can pursue other activities and still acknowledge his affection. They also consider the possibility that they were projecting their own desires onto the other partner.

AL: Maybe it's less threatening for me to see you as the one who wants attention, instead of acknowledging my own desire for closeness, because I don't want to become too dependent on our relationship.

MIKE: When I see you as the one who's more independent, I'm less aware of my own desire for other activities, and I can use our relationship as an excuse not to pursue my interests.

They realize that Al's desire for time alone doesn't mean he wants out of the relationship, and Mike's desire to connect doesn't mean he can't tolerate separate activities. They affirm their caring for each other, and negotiate a solution that takes them both into account.

Mike would like to have dinner together, and Al would like to watch the news. Underlying desires include wanting to connect and wanting time to oneself. A possible solution might be for Al to unwind when he comes home from work, catch the news, and they could have dinner together later.

Identifying Patterns[3]

More important, of course, than this particular solution is their ability to talk about the dynamic that has developed between them, without blaming each other (or themselves). By identifying this pattern as an example of mutual influence, they're less likely to label Mike as manipulative and dependent, or Al as aloof and afraid of intimacy. Understanding their behavior as a response to the pattern that has developed between them, they are able to interrupt this cycle by talking about it.

Instead of competing with Al's other interests, Mike could say he'd like some attention. And instead of simply avoiding Mike by watching television, reading the newspaper, or going into another room, Al could say he'd like some time to himself. They can negotiate their desires, instead of acting out their usual roles and then reacting to each other.

Having time to himself allows Al to get in touch with his desire to be with Mike. And knowing they'll have time together later allows Mike to get in touch with his own desire for independent activity. When a similar dynamic comes up in the future (as it no doubt will), they may not recognize it at first, but they'll have some tools to figure out what's happening between them.

* * *

A Guide for Handling Patterns

At this point, let's summarize what we've developed so far as a guide for handling patterns in our relationships.

To identify the underlying source of the conflict:

1. Ask yourself whether you're judging yourself for "unacceptable" or "petty" feelings.
2. Use your annoyance with your partner as a signal that you've accommodated him without saying what you want.
3. Reclaim any feelings you may be projecting onto your partner.

To keep from escalating:

4. Talk *about* your feelings and your impulse, rather than just acting on them.

   For example, instead of trying to get Al's attention by competing with the television, Mike could say "I find myself competing with the TV, and realize I'd like some attention."

   And instead of withdrawing when he feels pressured, Al could say "I notice I'm withdrawing, so I must feel I've already accommodated you."
5. Identify the pattern, rather than getting into an argument.

   For example, instead of putting Al down for being "aloof," Mike could say "We seem to be having that problem again where I'm wanting attention when you'd rather be by yourself."

   And instead of putting Mike down for being "dependent," Al could say "We seem to be having that problem again where you want some attention when I'd rather be by myself."
6. Empathize with how hard it is to have this conflict, instead of becoming defensive.

   For example, instead of blaming Al for being "aloof" because he wants to withdraw, Mike could say "It must be a drag to feel pressured again."

   And instead of blaming Mike for being "dependent" because he wants attention, Al could say "Oh, you must feel neglected."

Just because Mike's able to say he wants some attention doesn't mean Al has to stop whatever he's doing and give it to him; and just because Al wants to be by himself doesn't mean Mike has to go away. Acknowledging their desires simply allows them to negotiate openly for what they want.

Let's see how Mike and Al could use this approach to identify their pattern (instead of acting it out) when a familiar conflict crops up on their vacation in southern France.

They've been together all week, going out for meals, visiting museums, and traveling from one resort to another. One morning in Nice, Al picks up a newspaper on their way to breakfast. They find a sidewalk café and order croissants and coffee. Al folds the paper and lays it on the table.

Mike realizes he's feeling neglected. But he thinks he's being petty to get on Al's case in the middle of a beautiful vacation. Still, he's tempted to compete with the newspaper by trying to be witty and entertaining. But he knows Al would likely ignore him, and then he'd feel hurt. So he decides to talk *about* his impulse, instead of just acting on it or withdrawing in silence.

MIKE: I feel a little weird bringing this up, since I know it's a sore point between us, but I found myself wanting to compete with the paper for your attention.

AL [sighs, thinking *Here we go again*]: So are we going to argue about this on our vacation?

MIKE: Well, I figured I shouldn't say anything. But then I thought, instead of trying to compete for your attention, maybe we could see it as a signal.

AL [wary of being accused]: A signal for what?

MIKE: Well, we've been together constantly all week.

AL: So?

MIKE: So maybe you could use some time to yourself.

AL [still cautious, remembering their previous battles]: Well maybe. I admit I felt a twinge of guilt when I bought the paper, since it's our vacation and all.

MIKE: And we're supposed to be romantic twenty-four hours a day, and never be bored.

AL [laughing]: Right!

They both admit that being together constantly has been a strain. They realize how many unspoken compromises they've made over different interests while traveling together, because it's their long-awaited vacation. Both felt guilty for wanting some time apart, and it's a relief finally to talk about it.

Mike took a risk in bringing up a sensitive topic. It still irritates him when Al reads or watches TV during meals. But by talking *about* their tendency to get into an argument over this issue (or to withdraw from each other in boredom), they were able to identify their unspoken accommodations and avoid their usual argument. Instead, they have a very animated discussion over breakfast about feelings of guilt and obligation in their respective families. That afternoon, Mike goes to the museum, while Al goes off to the flea market; and they both look forward to getting together later for a swim.

As mentioned earlier, many conflicts can be resolved by going through the Six-Step Program for Resolving Conflicts outlined in chapter 4. But when you find yourselves caught in a cycle where your views of the problem are mutually disconfirming, look for unspoken accommodations, patterns of mutual influence, and consider the possibility that you're projecting some of your own needs and feelings onto your partner. This will help you see how you've both contributed to the pattern that has developed between you. Talking about the pattern, rather than acting it out, can help you interrupt this cycle.

Questions and Comments

Q: I'd feel overwhelmed trying to figure out the underlying function of every conflict.

A: Resolution of the surface problem often takes care of the underlying issue as well, without ever making it all that explicit. For example, an argument over "squeezing the toothpaste tube in the middle" could lead to a discussion about control in your relationship—or you could each buy your own tube of toothpaste. You don't have to analyze every interaction to find its deeper meaning, but it helps to have some tools for figuring out what the true issues are when you feel emotionally torn by a seemingly minor dispute.

Q: Bringing up sensitive issues seems like asking for trouble.

Are you saying you should never accommodate your lover or ignore petty annoyances?

A: We all let minor irritations go by at times. It's not a question of whether you "should" bring up issues that bother you. What's important is to be aware of the consequences of holding back. It may be riskier to let things build up to the point where you're so fed up you're no longer willing to negotiate.

You may not want to talk about a problem until you've sorted through your feelings first. You can also wait until you're both in a more relaxed mood, or you may want to see if you feel any differently about it later. It's possible to bring up an issue in a manner that indicates your willingness to take your partner's feelings into consideration as well. Chances are he's not oblivious to your discomfort, and it may be a relief to get things out in the open.

Q: I understand how accusing each other of being "dependent" or "aloof" just makes people defensive. But don't you think some men really are afraid of intimacy? And some men are too dependent?

A: While "dependency" and a "fear of intimacy" may seem like real issues in a relationship, we don't gain much by seeing either tendency as a pathological trait or a permanent part of one's personality. Instead, we can understand a move toward closeness or distance as a function of mutual influence within a relationship.

"Fear of intimacy" is often a sense of inadequacy in handling conflict. The one who withdraws does so partly because he doesn't know how to talk about his feelings or needs without feeling guilty or becoming defensive. When he learns how to assert himself, he's less likely to withdraw, and his partner will feel less deprived.

Likewise, what we call "dependency" is frequently a response to emotional abandonment. The one who feels deprived tries to compel his partner's attention, which in turn provokes further withdrawal. He can interrupt this cycle by talking about his desire for contact, instead of competing with his partner's other interests. Then they can negotiate a level of contact that suits them both.

P A R T

2

MAKING
IT WORK

We two boys together clinging,
One the other never leaving . . .
            —WALT WHITMAN, CALAMUS

6

Dealing with Differences

When we enter a relationship, we bring along a whole set of
assumptions about what intimacy means. We derive many of
our expectations from how we were raised in our own families,
and also from our class, ethnic, and religious backgrounds. As
gay men, we've also made some conscious decisions about how
we want to live; but sometimes we're not even aware of our own
expectations until we encounter a difference in our partner.

We may experience the difference as a purposeful violation,
rather than understanding that he may simply be operating from
a different set of expectations. In this chapter we'll look at some
issues that may arise in cross-cultural relationships, lifestyle
differences, and deciding to move in together. At the end we'll
also look at how to deal with differences in facing homophobic
discrimination.

Cultural Differences

Much cultural and ethnic diversity exists among gay men, though
it tends to be overlooked in the media. In a multiethnic society
such as ours, the potential for cross-cultural misunderstandings
is high. Entering a relationship is like entering a different culture,
even if we come from similar backgrounds. When we consider
the different norms developed in every family, to say nothing of

class, politics, and religion, it's a wonder we can communicate at all without constantly violating each other's norms.[1]

Some ethnic groups are not accustomed to disclosing feelings or openly discussing differences. There are many face-saving devices by which each person knows when to back off without being openly confronted. When everyone within the culture understands the unspoken norms, there's less of a need to be verbally explicit. In the United States we have so many different groups that we've needed to develop our skills in cross-cultural communication. The following example takes a look at how identifying cultural differences can clarify a misunderstanding about expressing affection.

Affection in Public

Julio, who grew up in Guatemala, recently started dating Kyle, who is American-born Chinese. One morning, while walking down the street, Julio touches Kyle's elbow and points out the buds starting to blossom on a tree. Kyle looks but moves his arm away. At the corner, waiting for the signal to change, Julio rests his hand on Kyle's shoulder, and Kyle shrugs him off. Looking in a store window, Julio puts his arm around Kyle's waist and bumps his hip. Kyle squirms away from him.

Julio wonders why Kyle is rejecting his affection; he was so tender when they made love the previous night. Meanwhile, Kyle questions whether he can have any space to himself.

JULIO: Why do you keep pushing me away?

KYLE: I'm not used to someone coming on to me all the time.

JULIO: I was just being affectionate. Why didn't you just say I was bothering you?

KYLE: Can't you take a hint? [Kyle feels annoyed and Julio feels hurt. But instead of assuming that Kyle has lost interest in him, Julio realizes this conflict may be a clue that they grew up with different norms for expressing affection.]

JULIO: I feel hurt and you seem annoyed. I wonder if we're experiencing some cultural differences?

KYLE: Like what?

JULIO: Well, how we were brought up. When I was a kid, all

my brothers and sisters would pile together on the sofa to watch *novelas* on TV. Touching doesn't mean I'm coming on to you.

KYLE: My family never expressed physical affection. No one's really ever touched me before, unless we were making love. Besides, I don't feel comfortable being affectionate right on the street.

JULIO: In our town in Guatemala, the girls held hands and the boys wrapped their arms over each other's shoulders as we circled the *zócalo,* our central plaza. We'd lean against the wall, holding a friend, and no one thought we were gay.

KYLE: I grew up in the suburbs of L.A., and if you even brushed against another guy he'd call you queer.

JULIO: It must have felt uncomfortable for me to touch you in public.

KYLE: Yes. I can't really enjoy physical contact when I'm constantly looking around to see if it's safe.

JULIO: So that's why you shrugged me off?

KYLE: I didn't say anything because you don't confront someone directly. People are supposed to notice if something bothers you.

JULIO: In my family you'd get run over if you didn't speak up.

KYLE: And in mine you weren't supposed to burden others with your feelings.

No one ever put into words what the norms were in either family—Julio and Kyle simply experienced them while growing up. By talking about their differences, Julio is less likely to interpret Kyle's behavior as a rejection, and Kyle is less likely to react by avoiding him.

Foreign Relations

Fabio, a student from Brazil in his last semester at college, has become involved with Tom, a leader of the Gay and Lesbian Alliance. Together, they planned a dance at school and a rally during AIDS Awareness Week. Over the months they've grown very attached—at least, Tom was under that impression. He's aware that Fabio's student visa will expire soon, and wonders how they'll be able to stay together:

TOM: What's going to happen to us?

FABIO: I'll see you sometime on business trips, and you could come down for Carnaval.

TOM: *Business* trips! I thought you were going to stay here.

FABIO: You know I can't stay. My visa's expiring—

TOM: We'll find a way—you could go to grad school, or work under the table. We'll get by somehow.

FABIO: What kind of life is that? I want to pursue my career, not be some dishwasher. I want to have a family—

TOM: I'm your family!

FABIO: You are very sweet. But I must get married, have children— [Tom stares incredulously.] Oh, don't look at me that way.

TOM: You can just say good-bye and pretend nothing has happened between us?

FABIO: I will always remember you—

TOM: How can you talk like this? Did the last eight months mean nothing to you?

FABIO: Of course, I'm very fond of you—

TOM: Then stay here. Or let me come with you.

FABIO: No, that's impossible.

TOM: Why? Don't you want me?

FABIO: It's simply not possible for me to live this way.

TOM: Why not?

FABIO: No, no, you have to accept. I'm becoming a man, I must get married for my family.

TOM: But you're gay!

FABIO: Tommy, you make this so difficult for me. This gay life is fun, it's for boys, but it's not real life.

TOM: Fabio, I know you are with me. Don't tell me you don't love me, you don't respond to my touch—

FABIO: It's just not my way. I can't stay here, and you can't come with me to Brazil.

TOM: There are plenty of gay men in Brazil. You told me yourself.

FABIO: But most have families. The ones who don't—well, they live on the fringe. I can't be a go-go boy the rest of my life, and neither can you. There are things I must accomplish—

TOM: Me too! But I want to accomplish them with you.

*   *   *

Fabio has fastened on to a solution—go back to Brazil, get married, and continue with his family's business. Underlying this solution is the desire to assume a role that meets the expectations of his class and family background. Tom wishes they could figure out some way they could still maintain their relationship, but Fabio has made other choices. In order to negotiate a solution that will work for both of them, Fabio must acknowledge the importance of their relationship, which (at least at this point) he's unwilling to do.

Another way they might approach this conflict is to acknowledge their difference. Tom can listen to Fabio's desire to be with his family and pursue his career. And Fabio can empathize with Tom's desire to continue their relationship. Rather than polarizing with Tom by justifying his decision to leave, he's more likely to get in touch with his own feelings of affection.

TOM: It's hard for you to reconcile your feelings for me with your obligations to your family.

FABIO: I shall really miss you, Tommy. You don't know how very difficult this is for me.

TOM: I want to convince you to stay, but it seems as if your mind is already made up.

FABIO: I thought we could be sweet together and then we'd have to say good-bye. I wanted just a fling, but I've grown to love you, Tommy.

TOM: The choice seems too hard for you.

FABIO: Why should we have to choose? That's why I wanted to go. I don't want to hurt you anymore. But I can't see any other way.

Because Tom is willing to empathize with his dilemma, Fabio is able to get in touch with his ambivalence. Fabio was trying to save them both from more heartache by pretending that their relationship wasn't that important. By exploring their feelings for each other, Fabio begins to think about whether satisfying his family's expectation that he will marry and take over the family business is more important to him than continuing his relationship with Tom. He may still decide to return to Brazil, but at least they will both be clear about his choice, rather than pretending they didn't really care about each other.

Lifestyle Differences

Not only do many men have cross-cultural relationships, they sometimes get involved with men from different class backgrounds. Some partners also have a considerable age difference between them. Class and generational differences can contribute to lifestyle conflicts that a couple must come to terms with. Housing, food, music, vacations, entertainment, socializing with friends, expectations about family involvement, and working out financial agreements are just a few of the areas that men with different social backgrounds must come to terms with. Being able to make room for our differences without judging each other is a significant task for any couple, especially for men who come from such different backgrounds. In the next example we'll look at how Denny and Charles deal with their large difference in income.

Denny grew up in a lower-middle-class Jewish neighborhood in New York. He was the first one in his family to go to college, where he lived in collective households. Since finishing school, he has worked for a food co-op and volunteered at the AIDS hotline. His lover, Charles, is fifteen years older, and grew up in Palos Verdes Estates in southern California. Well established in his banking career, he collects antiques and enjoys entertaining and traveling.

Charles has bought a lot of things for the house, which Denny could not afford and would never have considered buying himself. Charles feels resentful because Denny doesn't seem to care as much about the house as he does and never has enough money to join him on vacations to Europe and Asia. Denny likes what he does and has no desire to change jobs. Though he does benefit from having nice things around, and he'd like to go on some trips with Charles, he doesn't want to sacrifice his job and community interests by trying to earn enough money to keep up with Charles's lifestyle.

Using the steps for resolving conflicts outlined in chapter 4, they try to approach this lifestyle difference.

*   *   *

1a. Say What You'd Like

CHARLES: I'd like you to get a better-paying job.

DENNY: I'd like you to stop pressuring me to make as much money as you.

With the problem stated this way, they're at loggerheads over one particular solution. Instead of getting into a debate about whether Denny should get another job to make more money, they try to identify the desires that underlie this conflict.

1b. Distinguish Desires from Potential Solutions

What is it that Charles really wants? He says he wants Denny to earn more money, but why? What would more money enable them to do that they can't do now? By examining his assumptions, he is able to get more in touch with his desires.

CHARLES: I guess I'd like some nicer things around the house; but more important than that, I wish you'd come with me on my vacations. But you never have enough money to join me.

DENNY: I like the work I do, even if it doesn't make much money. Anyway, all your cruises are too expensive. You never want to do anything simple, like camping.

Because Charles implied that the reason they couldn't vacation together was that Denny didn't have enough money, he got a defensive response. At this point, Charles might assume Denny is being uncooperative and say "Sorry I brought it up—*my* idea of a vacation is *not* going off to lie in the *dirt*." But he thinks for a moment and realizes that Denny probably became defensive because he felt blamed. All Denny could hear was that he wasn't making enough money, not that Charles would like him to join him. So Charles tries again.

CHARLES: Well if you'd like to plan something together, maybe we could figure out a trip that we would both enjoy. I imagine there's something between camping in the desert and Club Med.

DENNY: Well sure. I never knew you'd settle for anything less.

Instead of demanding that Denny earn more money in order to join him on a vacation that Charles has already planned, Charles suggests that they plan something together. Denny says he'd like to join him. Now they can separate potential solutions from their underlying desires.

Potential solution	*Underlying desire*
Get another job	Vacation together

1c. Identify Behaviors and Feelings; Listen and Reflect

CHARLES: I guess in the past when you've said it's just not worth it to you to earn enough money to join me, I felt hurt, assuming you meant *I* wasn't important enough for you to bother.

DENNY: You felt hurt because you thought I didn't really want to go with you? [He reflects Charles's feelings.]

CHARLES: Yes. I wanted to know that maybe I was worth some extra effort.

DENNY: It was more because I never felt included. It was *your* vacation, not anything we planned together. And I felt angry when you suggested I get another job, because it seemed that you didn't really respect my work.

CHARLES [reflects]: My pressuring you to make more money seemed as if I was putting down the co-op?

DENNY: Yes.

CHARLES: I've also wondered whether you were judging me for being a banker.

Each partner had assumed the other was judging him, which left them both feeling defensive. Neither wanted to be put down for his work, or his taste in vacations, so it was hard to admit they would like to do something together. By identifying their underlying desires, they were able to shift from "Why doesn't Denny earn more money?" and go on to brainstorm "How could we vacation together?"

*   *   *

Moving in Together

The issue of whether to live together is a major decision for many couples. It's helpful to clarify your expectations about emotional commitment, as well as practical considerations.[2] Accommodating each other's habits and preferences can take a lot of adjustments, especially if you've been living on your own. In the following example we'll look at how Sal and Eric deal with a difference they encounter a month after Sal moves in with Eric.

One night after dinner, Sal says he'd like to make the den into his own room. Eric is taken aback by this news; their sexual relations have slowed down to two or three times a week, but he hasn't noticed any decrease in their affection. He likes "spooning" all through the night.

ERIC: Is there anything wrong? Am I snoring, or stealing the blankets?

SAL: It's not that; it's just—well, before I moved in we slept together when we both wanted to, but now we end up in the same bed every night.

ERIC: You don't want to sleep with me?

SAL [realizing that Eric is hurt, he tries to reassure him]: I still love you and want to be with you, but sometimes I like to sleep by myself.

ERIC: Do you need more room?

SAL: That's part of it; that double bed is pretty small. Plus I've had trouble sleeping with you glommed on to me all night.

ERIC: I thought you liked spooning.

SAL: I do after we've made love, but then I need to stretch out.

ERIC: What if we got a king-size bed, and you let me know when you need more space?

SAL: That would help. But I think I'd also like my own room. When we had our own apartments, I went out of my way to see you. After moving in together, I lose myself sometimes. I want to miss you occasionally.

ERIC [reflecting what he has understood and saying how he feels]: I feel hurt and a little threatened. I understand your desire to sleep together when you "miss" me—but I'm sure I'd miss you every night. I guess I'm a little scared you're not as interested in me.

Sal reassures Eric that he does love him, and that his desire for his own room doesn't reflect a lack of interest: "I'm sure we'd still end up sleeping together most of the time. But I'd also like to have some space I've fixed up myself and made into my own room. It still feels like I'm staying over in your apartment. I want it to feel like my home, too."

At this point they're ready to differentiate potential solutions from their underlying desires.

Potential solution	Underlying desires
Sal has his own room.	Enough space in bed. Make the apartment Sal's home, too. Have some time apart. Eric needs some reassurance.

They go on to brainstorm ways of taking care of Sal's desire to have his own room while still affirming their emotional closeness and sexual interest:

Get a king-size bed.

Turn den into bedroom for Sal.

Sal could have some say about the layout and arrangement of the rest of the apartment.

Sal could be clear about when he needs more space in bed, and not store up resentment.

Eric could back off a little to give Sal more emotional space.

Sal could initiate contact to reassure Eric.

They decide to get a king-size bed and to be clearer about the amount of physical closeness they want when they sleep together. Sal makes the den into his room, and they negotiate bringing some of Sal's furniture and paintings into the living room. Once Sal has his own room, he is able to get in touch again with his fondness for Eric and his desire for intimate contact.

Facing Discrimination

Many of the difficulties we face as gay couples derive from living in a homophobic society. Constantly gauging how safe it is to acknowledge our relationships can be a strain. We may have some differences over when to express affection in public, be open about being gay, or object to homophobic remarks. The one who is more open may label the other as homophobic, or judge him for not taking as many risks. And the one who prefers not to make his sexual orientation an issue can see his partner as insensitive and controlling. After a number of arguments, they may then refuse to discuss it, and be tempted to make their own social arrangements without taking the other into consideration. In the following example with Brad and Joel, we'll see how Brad can get support for his dilemma about coming out at work instead of trying to hide it.

Brad works for a firm that is having its annual holiday party, and "significant others" are invited. He tells Joel he'd rather go by himself, as he wouldn't want to subject him to a boring office party. Joel says he thought Brad liked some of the people he worked with; he's always talking about Sherry and Rex, and Joel would like to meet them.

Brad says they could meet some other time, but Joel is suspicious. "You've worked there two years now, but we've never had them over."

Brad says, "I'd just as soon keep my work and social life separate."

Since he's not openly gay at work, Brad suspects that his job would be in jeopardy if he brought Joel along. And because Joel is "out" practically everywhere, Brad assumes that Joel would judge him for not being open at work. He insists office parties are boring, rather than telling Joel the real reason he doesn't want him to come. Because Brad doesn't say what he's really concerned about, Joel wonders whether Brad is ashamed of their relationship. If Joel doesn't disclose his fear, either, they could both make assumptions that are left unchallenged: Brad assumes Joel would judge him, and Joel assumes Brad is ashamed of him.

Instead, Joel says, "I was wondering if you really feel comfortable introducing me to your straight friends."

This allows Brad to realize the effect of his secretiveness. "Well, it's not that I'm ashamed of you. It's hard for me to admit it, but I've never come out at work."

JOEL: So that's it. You thought I'd judge you for staying in the closet.

BRAD: Well you're Mr. "Come out, come out, wherever you are."

JOEL: I suppose whether you're out at work doesn't really affect me. But I want to hear more about how dangerous you think it is to be open at work. Don't you think they already suspect?

Because Joel spoke up, Brad was able to reassure him that his decision was not discounting their relationship. Brad goes on to describe the homophobic atmosphere at work, and Joel understands his decision as an acknowledgment of the level of oppression that he experiences in his job.

When partners polarize over a problem, they tend to reinforce each other's rigidity in maintaining a certain position. Seeing Joel as the one who is "always out" and Brad as the one who is "always closeted" removes both men's flexibility in their willingness to consider alternative approaches to the problem. But when Joel empathizes with Brad's dilemma, rather than judging him for it, Brad may be willing to reconsider how accurate his perceptions are about being more open at work.

Whenever you empathize with your partner, he'll be more willing to explore his own ambivalence about the problem, instead of polarizing with you. Brad no longer sees Joel's position as something he needs to defend against in order to maintain his own self-esteem. Instead, he begins to see Joel as an ally in helping him figure out whether he wants to come out at work.

Exercise

When you encounter a difference with your partner, you may be tempted to argue, or point out logical fallacies in his assumptions. This can lead to rigidifying your positions, rather than helping you understand each other. Instead of trying to dispute each other's opinions, it's helpful to listen and try to understand how you feel.

For this exercise in clarifying values, first try comparing responses to a movie, play, or TV show. There's nothing to solve in this discussion; it's simply an exercise to see what it's like to really understand another person's point of view.

People often discuss film in a competitive way. We judge the acting, the plot, and technical devices. We argue about whether the movie is boring, exciting, stupid, or engaging. We often imply that anyone who doesn't agree with us is boring or stupid, as well. But instead of judging the film (or each other), talk about how you were affected by it. How did you feel? What was it about this movie that you could relate to, or that put you off? You may still want to challenge each other's ideas in a friendly debate, but hold off until you've both had a chance to talk about the film and reflect your responses.

Everyone has heard the saying "You can't argue politics or religion." Most people have such strong feelings about these beliefs (in families, especially) that it's often considered rude even to acknowledge our differences. We're not sure how to talk about beliefs without making judgments. Of course, many beliefs *are* judgments about what we think is right or wrong. Yet it's possible to discuss our differences in a noncompetitive way, without judging each other.

Rather than take your partner's beliefs as a challenge to yours, you can be curious about each other's upbringing and experience. Talk about your feelings while growing up, significant events that influenced your beliefs, and what they mean to you now. Rather than establishing the "truth," or even trying to reach an agreement, you can simply learn more about how you each experience the world. It's possible to feel closer for having explored your beliefs, rather than alienated and threatened.

Next, pick a difference that affects a decision in your relationship. Use the steps from chapter 4 to clarify your difference and identify underlying desires. See whether you can make room for both of you to express your preferences. As with previous exercises, it's helpful to begin with an example that's not the most pressing conflict in your relationship. Small successes can give you the confidence to move on to more crucial issues: how you deal with money, where you want to live, how open you are about being gay, or how you relate to friends and family.

*　*　*

Living with the Difference

What attracts you to each other may be very similar to the qualities that drive you crazy. You like how stable and self-contained your partner is, but he doesn't like to go out, have friends over, or say how he feels. He's gregarious, funny, and entertaining, but so many guys are hanging on him that you feel competitive for his attention. He's very caring, but spends a lot of time caring for other friends instead of you. You admire his intellectual, creative, or professional achievements, but miss him when he travels. It's doubtful you'll find anyone who totally meets all your expectations, and it's unlikely you will change your partner's basic personality.

You may also have very different ways of seeing the world. Differences can enrich your relationship, as well as being a source of tension. You can understand each other's beliefs and cultural norms without needing to convert your partner to your point of view. It's often useful to look at what *difference* the difference makes—is there any particular reason why you can't coexist with opposing views? Sometimes couples simply agree to disagree on certain matters. Try brainstorming ways to accommodate your differences. When you compare your feelings and experiences, you may learn another way of looking at certain issues you've never thought of before; and you also find out more about each other—how you were affected by your past, what really matters to you, and what you hope for in the future.

Questions and Comments

Q: My boyfriend is rather flamboyant, and doesn't hesitate to let anyone know he's "queer." If someone makes a catcall from a passing car, he'll yell back at them. While I admire his courage, I don't think it's safe. You never know what kind of nut might pull out a gun and shoot you.

A: Listen to him, and find out more about his history and how gratifying it is for him to yell back at "queer baiters." Rather than arguing about whether his behavior is the best way to counteract homophobic remarks, you can say what you're afraid of. This will help him understand how his behavior affects you. By understanding how you arrived at your different styles of dealing with homophobic taunts, you may be able to brainstorm ways of handling these situations that take both of you into consideration.

Q: My lover is disabled and uses a wheelchair. I'm more than willing to help out with his care, though sometimes I get tired of all the effort it takes to clean up and get ready to go anywhere. He tries to take care of me by not making too many demands, and then I get confused trying to figure out what he really wants.

A: You may feel guilty for wishing you didn't have to take care of your partner, and he may be trying not to be a burden on you. Realistically, you *won't* be able to do it all, and you need help. You'll end up feeling worn out, resentful, and distant from each other if you never acknowledge the effort it takes (on the part of both of you) to deal with his disability.

We tend to assume that we can't ask for what we want for fear of being too demanding. But you can both say what you want and still negotiate. If he'd like to go out but you're too tired, think of other ways to meet both of your desires, such as calling a friend or getting some attendant care. You can also plan for the fact that you'll need some assistance by making arrangements ahead of time.

7

Sexual Communication

The heart has its reasons that reason knows not of.
—PASCAL

Intimate relationships are based on emotional ties, such as love, affection, and sexual attraction. Though some men experience sex as more of a physical need, distinct from emotional expression, sexual relations can carry a wealth of intimate associations and feelings: affirming male bonding, love and appreciation, giving and receiving pleasure, expressing vulnerability and caring, as well as sexual excitement.

Sexual Availability

As men we've been socialized to be "ready and willing" at any moment, and this can create unrealistic expectations about our availability for sexual relations. We may find it easier to have sex, for example, than to admit our desire for attention or comfort. Passion isn't the only way to express love, and affection needn't lead to orgasm, when what we really want at the moment is simply to be held.

It may also be difficult to say we don't feel like having sex. But we communicate so much nonverbally that it's usually obvious when we're not making love with much enthusiasm. When you admit that you're not in the mood for sex, it can be a relief to feel understood by your partner. Not feeling pressured to perform may allow you to feel closer emotionally, or even to become aroused after all.

You can distinguish between stimulation that's headed toward orgasm and more relaxed contact (though one can easily lead to the other). You may not feel sexual initially, but become aroused in response to your partner's passion. You can work out agreements about when "no" really means "no" and when you are playfully inviting seduction. Initiating or declining sex doesn't always have to be verbal, of course. You may be half asleep when your partner begins to fondle you or thrust against you. If you'd rather be left alone at the moment, you might take his wandering hand and wrap his arm around your waist as you fall back to sleep.

You can also let your lover know what you like by making appreciative sounds or guiding him into positions, pressures, or rhythms you prefer. Touching him as you'd like to be touched is one way of expressing your preference, though this can still lead to miscommunication. If he's handling you roughly and you like a soft touch, you may stroke him more gently; meanwhile, he'd like you to be firmer, so he grabs you harder. Rather than assuming that your partner isn't very perceptive or responsive, you can also realize you're simply not getting your message across, in which case it helps to talk about it.

Communicating clearly about your preferences can prevent you from making false assumptions about your differences in sexual availability. You can appreciate your partner's sexual attentions, let him know what you want, and be sensitive to each other's feelings. At the end of this chapter we'll look at some other ways to enhance sexual contact in gay relationships.

Decline in Frequency

Male couples often wonder if something's wrong when they don't make love as often as they used to. Yet most couples experience a decline in sexual frequency over the life of their relationship. This happens not just with male couples, but with lesbian and heterosexual couples as well.[1]

McWhirter and Mattison attribute a decrease in sexual activity to the establishment of familiarity and comfort in gay relationships.[2] We might also see this decline as a natural shift toward a depth of loving that doesn't always need to be expressed genitally.

This decrease is also influenced by the natural aging process: it takes longer and we need more physical stimulation to become erect; our erections are not as full or as hard; it takes longer to ejaculate; it takes longer after ejaculation to become erect again; ejaculations become less powerful; and we ejaculate less frequently.[3] None of this means, of course, that we can't have satisfying sexual relations well into old age. And we needn't think of sex only in terms of ejaculating, when our whole bodies can respond to each other's touch throughout our lives.

A decrease in sexual relations may be more difficult for male couples to accommodate than for heterosexual or lesbian couples, because of the emphasis on sex in the gay male culture. It helps to say how you feel about these changes. A decline in frequency needn't reflect a lack of interest in your relationship, or indicate that you feel any less deeply about each other.

Safer Sex

The onslaught of AIDS has dramatically altered the lifestyle of sexual openness that developed after Stonewall. Our struggle to liberate homosexual relations from social ostracism and self-condemnation has been challenged on many fronts; our community has been devastated by the loss of thousands of lives.

You may have resigned yourself to the necessity of having safer sex but feel self-conscious about bringing it up. If your favorite ways to have sex now seem dangerous, you may feel demoralized and withdraw from sexual activity altogether. If you're unwilling to talk about it because you feel too vulnerable, your lover may interpret your withdrawal as rejection. The isolation and frustration resulting from such a withdrawal can lead to an impulse to indulge in unsafe sex anyway.

We've responded to the epidemic in a variety of ways: some men prefer to get to know each other before becoming sexually involved, and some men have retreated from sexuality altogether, figuring they'll eventually have a monogamous relationship or nothing. And others have been exploring how to nurture one another through massage and safe sex with friends as well as lovers.

In safe sex workshops across the country, men are discussing how the loss of a more carefree lifestyle has influenced their sexual interests. We can affirm our sexuality and still take care of one another by learning how to eroticize safer sex.[4]

Guidelines for Safer Sex

The following guidelines have been derived from the information currently available about safer sex.[5]

Unsafe
Any practice that allows blood or semen to enter the other person's body can transmit the AIDS virus:

Unprotected anal (or vaginal) intercourse
Ejaculating into the mouth
Unprotected fisting
Sharing sex toys
Sharing needles
Sharing razors

While the virus has been isolated in saliva, and may be present in any other body secretion (urine, feces, sweat, and tears), these fluids have not been shown to be likely modes of transmissions. However, oral-anal contact (rimming) is a transmission route for many other diseases, such as hepatitis, amoebic dysentery, and parasites. Multiple infections can suppress your immune system, possibly making you more vulnerable to infection by the AIDS virus. For this reason, rimming is often listed as unsafe unless a barrier is used, such as a dental dam.

Unprotected fisting is considered unsafe because it can allow blood contact through small cuts and fissures.

Possibly Safe
These practices are considered possibly safe (or possibly unsafe):

Anal intercourse with a latex condom (and a *water-soluble* lubricant)
Oral sex prior to ejaculation

Deep kissing
Fisting with a latex glove

Latex condoms are necessary because animal skin condoms do not form an effective barrier to the AIDS virus. A water-soluble lubricant is needed because latex condoms are dissolved by oil and petroleum jelly–based products. A lubricant with nonoxynol-9 (a spermicide) is recommended because it can kill the AIDS virus.[6]

The above practices are considered only *possibly* safe because condoms and gloves can break, and even a lubricant with nonoxynol-9 cannot be depended on to provide a protective barrier. Withdrawal before ejaculating would be a safer way to use a condom. Oral sex is considered possibly safe because some men ooze "pre-cum" and semen before they ejaculate. Deep kissing may involve blood contact through bleeding gums or mouth sores.

Safe

Mutual masturbation
Rubbing against each other
Massage
Dry kissing
Not inserting head of penis into mouth during oral sex
Using a condom with oral sex
Anal insertion of finger with glove or condom

Remember that alcohol and other drugs affect your judgment. You may end up engaging in forms of sex outside your original agreement when you're high. Drugs and alcohol also impair the functioning of your immune system.

Negotiating Safer Sex

Before AIDS, our initial attractions often felt very spontaneous, unencumbered by verbal negotiations. An explicit discussion of what you like (and what feels safe to you) may not seem very romantic. You can still communicate a lot without having to say much, but these days it seems necessary for us to be more explicit, especially about safer sex, when entering a new relationship.

Some men prefer to talk about what they like before having sex. Others are aroused by sexual discussions, and feel comfortable being explicit with each other in bed. When you first meet someone, you may not feel comfortable sharing a complete rundown of your sexual history. Negotiations with a new partner can be fairly brief if you limit your contact to safe sex.

TIM: Let's be safe, all right?

JAY: Meaning . . . ?

TIM: I don't have a condom, so I'm not comfortable with anal sex, and I'd rather not suck each other off.

JAY: Sure, that's fine with me.

If you're interested in a longer-term relationship, you may choose to disclose more about yourself and want to know more about him: what sorts of practices you've engaged in, whether you've taken the HIV test, or your current health status. This knowledge may help you assess your willingness to engage in possibly safe practices.

In negotiations over possibly safe sex, the issue of trust arises—will he be able to let you know when he's about to come, so he doesn't ejaculate in your mouth? You've agreed to have anal sex with a condom if he pulls out before he ejaculates—do you feel confident he will?

TIM: I feel comfortable sucking you off if you let me know when you're about to come.

JAY: Okay.

While having sex, we respond to each other physically, emotionally, and erotically. It can feel irritating to have to switch from the passion of making love to think about whether you're still being safe. Sadness and anger about our loss of sexual spontaneity and freedom are understandable. It's helpful to say how you feel about having to deal with safe sex, so you're less likely to take out your frustrations on each other.

TIM: Whoops—it slipped off. Hold on; I've got it. [He pulls out and lies next to Jay.]

JAY: What a drag; I was right on the verge.

TIM: You miss the good old days?

JAY: Yeah, I do.

TIM: Me too. I've got another rubber—

JAY [glancing over at Tim]: Looks like you'll need some help getting it on.

TIM: Will you help me rise to the occasion?

A little humor can also keep us from taking sex (or ourselves) too seriously.

As safer sex becomes the norm, sexual contact will feel more spontaneous again. You won't have to talk much about what you want if you've already reached some agreements about the kind of sex you feel comfortable with.

HIV Testing

John and Brian have had a monogamous relationship for a number of years. They got together when the news about AIDS was first coming out. By the time people started taking safer sex seriously, they'd already had unprotected anal intercourse for a long time. Then Stuart, John's former lover, told him he came out positive on the AIDS antibody test. Now Brian feels uncomfortable not using a condom. He hesitates to bring up his fears, not wanting to bother John while he's upset over Stuart. But John notices the difference in their sex life, and wonders what's wrong.

JOHN: You don't seem to be as enthused about getting it on lately. Is something bothering you?

BRIAN: Stuart's news got me to thinking about us.

JOHN: I thought so. You're wondering if we've been exposed?

BRIAN: Yeah. Do you think it would help to use a condom at this point?

JOHN: Sort of like closing the barn door after the horses have fled.

BRIAN [laughing]: Really. But they say multiple exposures can make a difference.

JOHN: Assuming either of us has been exposed.

BRIAN: I've been thinking about taking the test.

JOHN: You mean, *the* test?

BRIAN: Yeah.

JOHN: How would you feel it it came out positive?

BRIAN: I'd be devastated.

JOHN: So why do it?

BRIAN: I'm too nervous not knowing.

JOHN: Well, if you do it, I don't want to know about it.

BRIAN: You're not ready to deal with it, huh?

JOHN: Definitely not.

BRIAN: But I wouldn't want to find out by myself.

JOHN: You're really worried about this, aren't you?

BRIAN: Yeah, I am.

JOHN: I need a while to think about this. But I'd be willing to use condoms in the meantime.

BRIAN: All right. I'd feel a lot more comfortable.

Guidelines for HIV Testing

When the antibody test first became available, many men were reluctant to take it because they assumed there wasn't much they could do about a positive test except feel anxious. Now some treatments are available for men who are HIV positive but have no other symptoms. More men are taking the test in the hope that a full-blown case of AIDS might be prevented.[7] If you're considering taking the AIDS antibody test, it's important to:

1. Talk with your lover, friends, or a counselor about your reasons for taking the test.
2. Say what you think your results might be.
3. Imagine how you would feel if the test came out either positive or negative.
4. Discuss your decision with your physician. Decide whether you wish to take the test *anonymously,* at an alternative test site, so your results won't become part of your medical record.
5. Have your support system in place before you take the test: your partner, friends, or counselor should know when you're getting the results, and be available to help you process this information. (See chapter 10, "When a Lover Has AIDS," for a discussion of how you can give each other support when you or your partner is infected with HIV.)

It's still not considered absolutely safe even for two "negatives" to have unprotected sex, unless neither of you has ever had sex (or shared needles) with anyone else. Though most people produce antibodies within six months of infection, it can take much longer, so it's possible to obtain a false negative to the antibody test. Obviously, you need to consider your own sexual histories to figure out which practices you feel comfortable with.

It's vital for men who are seropositive (tested positive to the AIDS antibody) to have safe sex. Even if you've both been infected with HIV, multiple exposures can overwhelm your immune system. You also risk infection from cytomegalovirus, herpes, hepatitis, parasites, and other sexually transmitted diseases.

Sexual Dysfunction

The most common dysfunctions in men are not getting an erection (impotence), delayed ejaculation, and "premature" ejaculation. But how long you take to become aroused or reach orgasm is dysfunctional only insofar as it interferes with reaching a particular goal—such as being able to insert an erect penis somewhere, holding off an orgasm until you're both ready, and wanting to come. It's important to gauge this for yourselves, and not think you have to adapt to some arbitrary standard.

Dealing with an Absence of Erection
An inability to get an erection can be due to certain medical conditions (such as diabetes, vascular disease, and spinal cord injuries), medications (for anxiety, blood pressure, and antidepressants), and the use of alcohol and street drugs.[8] As mentioned earlier, our capacity for erections also lessens with age. If you've noticed a marked decline in your ability to get (or maintain) an erection, a medical examination can determine what is causing your difficulty. Most cases of physiologically based impotence can be treated successfully.[9] If you have erections in your sleep, upon awakening, or when you masturbate, chances are there's nothing wrong with the plumbing.

Most men experience occasions when they're not able to get or maintain an erection. The word "impotence," despite its connotation of lacking virility, simply means that you don't have an erection when you want one, or think you should have one. A vicious circle can arise for a man when he doesn't have an erection at some point, and then becomes self-conscious about the next time. He focuses his attention on his potential "failure," rather than on the actual sensations he's experiencing. His partner may become impatient with him, and this increases the pressure.

There can be all sorts of reasons why your penis doesn't feel like standing up. Maybe you're too cold; you're using too much tension in other muscles, trying to hold yourself in a certain position; you're tired; you drank too much; or you just ejaculated a few minutes ago. Your penis may be more in touch with how you feel than you are—perhaps you're not really in the mood, you're not feeling very trustful, or you're preoccupied with other thoughts or feelings. You may wish you were aroused so you could please your partner. But if he's as interested in you and how you feel as he is in what you can do with your penis, you won't feel so much pressure to perform.

The main problem with impotence that isn't physiologically based is *thinking* it's a problem. You try to do something that would happen spontaneously if you weren't making so much effort. The harder you try, the more aware you are of feeling frustrated. When you're not concentrating so hard on getting an erection, you can pay more attention to pleasurable sensations. Lying back and enjoying your mutual contact is more likely to arouse you than getting down on yourself for not getting it up.

One way of interrupting this circle is to agree beforehand not to engage in anal intercourse (or whatever sort of sex you enjoy that requires an erect penis). You can relax and play, do erotic massage, and not worry about whether you get an erection, because you're not going to do anything with it anyway. With low-pressure physical contact, you may become erect spontaneously. Following a few sessions of abstinence, you regain the confidence that your erection is going to stick around for a while.

Delayed Ejaculation

There's a combination of tension and relaxation in the buildup of sexual excitement that culminates in the physiological reflex of orgasm and ejaculation. When you try to force an orgasm, you're no longer in touch with the sensations that are likely to lead to one. If you let those sensations build in their intensity and excitement, you're more likely to come when you're ready. You don't have to have an orgasm every time you have sex, either; feeling comfortable with this can decrease your performance anxiety. Having sex less frequently, or not masturbating between contacts, may also allow you to come sooner.

Ejaculating "Too Soon"

"Premature" ejaculation means coming too soon—but "too soon" for whom? You may wish to last longer in order to feel a mounting of mutual pleasure with your partner. If you haven't had sex for a while, or you're especially excited, you may come fairly quickly with very little stimulation.

Part of the problem for some men (when it is a problem) is that they're not really aware of how turned on they are until they pass that magical moment of inevitability. They end up coming before they even realized they were on their way. Pay more attention to how stimulated you are, and slow things down before you're about to come. Practice getting very close to that moment and backing off. It can be fun to see how long you can keep each other on the verge of orgasm. You can also go ahead and come whenever you're ready. The second time around it will take longer to reach orgasm.

There are a couple of other ways to hold off ejaculating: one is the "squeeze technique," whereby you give an *erect* penis a healthy squeeze at the head, which can subdue one's headlong rush to ejaculate (not *too* hard, or you'll have to revive the poor fellow!).[10] The other method is less intrusive, because you don't need to withdraw your penis or interrupt sexual contact: press on the perineum (the area between your scrotum and anus) for a moment, and slow down your thrusting motions. You shouldn't try this if you've already started to come, because it will back up the flow of semen.[11]

If there's nothing wrong with you physiologically, and low-pressure sexual contact doesn't seem to help with any of these problems, you may have some conflicts you're not consciously aware of. Sex-related problems often represent a difficulty in communicating other emotional needs and desires. If you have some ambivalence about homosexual relations, or there's some tension in your relationship you're not acknowledging, it may express itself through any of these dysfunctions. It may be helpful to seek professional counseling in order to resolve your conflicts about sexual contact, or learn to deal more directly with feelings in your relationship.

Enhancing Sexual Relations

When things are going smoothly, you may not feel the need to talk about what you want sexually—you may be able to flow together and respond to nonverbal cues. But sometimes couples make assumptions about what each partner wants, because they've never really talked about their sexual preferences. It helps now and then to let each other know what you enjoy. Following are a few suggestions for enhancing your sexual relationship. See what else you come up with on your own!

Tell Each Other What You Like

Do you like sex in the morning, at night, or in the afternoon? How often do you like having sex, and in what setting? Men experience a wide variety of sexual arousal. There's no right or wrong way of having sex between consenting adults—you can find your own, mutually satisfying ways to stimulate each other. Set aside some time to tell each other what you especially enjoy. Emphasize what you appreciate about his attentions. Say what else you'd like that would be even more exciting.

Let each other know which activities you don't feel comfortable with. See if you can express your desires through mutual sexual contact. Then show each other what you like—take turns, and communicate through appreciative sounds, guiding each other into the rhythms, pressures, and motions you prefer. Afterward, tell your partner what you enjoyed, what doesn't work for you, and what else you'd like to try.

Interrupt Your Usual Routine

We get into a rut when we're tired or not feeling terribly imaginative, or when we already feel that we've explored the territory of each other's sexuality about as far as we can. Sometimes it helps to make some changes: a vacation is one way to freshen your approach to each other, but smaller changes in time, location, clothing, and style can create a slightly different dynamic that might be enough to arouse your interest.

The pull of outside relationships may be an expression of

your desire for mystery, intrigue, and surprise. Sometimes couples get into arguments just to create some tension, but there are other ways of getting enough distance from each other so you feel refreshed and intrigued when you get back together, such as having some of your own interests and outside activities and doing things with other friends.

Some couples experiment with erotic magazines and videos, or even three-ways. While outside stimulation may rekindle your interest in each other, erotica and other partners may also bring up feelings of inadequacy or jealousy that you hadn't anticipated. It's important to keep tabs on how these experiments affect you.

Increase Physical Tension
Doing some intense physical activity like sports, dance, working out at the gym, or even a construction project encourages mutual physical involvement. Sex doesn't always have to be mellow and romantic. For some men, testing their strength and striving against each other is sexually arousing. Some enjoy (consensual) restraints, and like to explore the line between pain and pleasure in sexual contact. It's important to keep communication very clear throughout such explorations, so you can let each other know when you've had enough.

Eroticize Your Body
Sometimes we become so oriented toward ejaculating that we neglect other erogenous zones: besides genitals, lips, and anus, explore the neck, ears, and nipples—don't forget the back of your knees, fingers, toes, and inner thighs. In fact, your whole body is an erogenous zone! Areas that we think of as ticklish (ribs, soles of feet, armpits) become very erotic when you relax and breathe into those highly charged sensations, spreading them throughout your body. Many people who have lost sensation in their genitals due to illness or injury have learned to experience a kind of orgasm in armpits, earlobes, nipples, and other areas.[12] Explore the possibilities of eroticizing your entire body.

Moods and Appreciation
A walk in the woods or by the ocean; dressing up and going out to dinner; making a fire; going camping; staying in a hotel; flowers, small gifts, and notes—use your imagination to create an atmo-

sphere that expresses your interest and appreciation. Nurture an element of surprise and endearing thoughtfulness in your relationship.

Sex and Affection

Experiment with connecting sex and affection, and also let your partner know when you just want to be held. Allow yourself occasionally to be sexual without having to ejaculate. Give each other both erotic and nonerotic massages. Reveal the hesitations that arise about becoming too close; likewise, tell him when you feel warm and loving, too!

Remember that feelings of intimacy can't be manufactured simply by increasing sexual acrobatics. We feel closer to each other when we talk about how we really feel. Once we've been acknowledged and appreciated, our sexual desire often follows.

Questions and Comments

Q: Since my lover wants sex more often than I do, he usually waits for me to initiate making love. But lately he's been refusing me, and says it's because I have more "power" in the relationship.

A: He may feel "one-down" because he's more likely to be rejected than you. Perhaps he's trying to redress an imbalance in your sexual relationship. However, withholding can easily lead to a stalemate in which you stop having sex altogether.

Levels of sexual passion may decline at different rates, and the one who wants sex more frequently can misinterpret this decline as a lack of interest and need some reassurance. If you're not interested in being sexual when he is, how would you feel about holding him while he stimulates himself? Find ways to affirm your affection, even if your frequency desires differ.

Q: My lover says he tested negative on the HIV antibody test. I'm hesitant to insist on safe sex because he might think I don't trust him.

A: It's important to take responsibility for our own sexual behavior. Insisting on safe sex needn't imply anything about the trustworthiness of your partner. What's important is your own safety and comfort level, regardless of his sexual history. If you feel uncomfortable bringing up this topic on your own, couples counseling can help you negotiate the kind of sexual contact you both feel comfortable with.

Q: When we tried using a condom, my lover lost his erection. Now he refuses to use one, and says if he can't have "real" sex, he'd rather not bother.

A: Many men lose their erection when they use a condom the first time. Their attention is diverted from pleasurable sensations by their anxiety over whether they'll still be able to function. It's nothing to be ashamed of, and it's no reflection on your masculinity or potency. Try making the condom part of your sexual experience, so you don't have to interrupt your lovemaking and then reposition yourself to have intercourse after you've slipped it on.

Some men who are disdainful of safer sex vacillate between abstinence and having unsafe sex. Your lover may be demoralized, angry, frightened, or frustrated. Talking about your feelings in response to the AIDS crisis will help you feel more like allies than adversaries. Then you can explore having sex in ways you both feel comfortable with.

Q: Having sex after an argument helps me feel better, but my lover refuses to touch me. Then I get mad because he's withholding sex to punish me.

A: Rather than interpreting his behavior as a punishment, it helps to understand your different approaches to making up after an argument. For you, having sex feels comforting and helps you feel closer, whereas your lover may need to recover from your quarrel *in order* to feel intimate. Once he feels acknowledged and understood, he may be open to having sex again. Try talking about this difference before you have another argument.

8

Monogamy versus an Open Relationship

Many male couples struggle with conflicting desires for stability in their relationship and their interest in outside sexual contacts. It's tempting to fasten on to either monogamy or an open relationship as a solution before we've taken the time to sort through our underlying desires. Looking at what we hope either monogamy or nonmonogamy would resolve in our relationships can help us identify what's really at the heart of this conflict.

In this chapter we'll follow a couple through their struggle to come to terms with this issue as an example of how you might approach similar negotiations, experiments, and feelings in your own relationship. But first let's look at some of our assumptions about monogamy and multiple partners in gay relationships.

Exclusivity and Commitment

To heterosexual couples, marriage usually implies sexual exclusivity in a committed, emotional bond. However, many cultures tolerate a double standard: the wife is expected to be "faithful" (in order to provide "legitimacy" to children) while the husband is free to have a mistress (or prostitutes) on the side. The wife, who usually knows about her husband's infidelity, suffers in silence, unless he rubs her face in his indiscretions, in which case she feels justified in making a scene. The husband may in fact be just as committed to the marriage as she is; he displays his remorse with some token of his devotion, and she forgives him. In the future, he tries to be more discreet.

This is obviously a caricature of marriage. But male conditioning also affects our expectations in gay relationships, where neither partner has been socialized to settle down. Our families, the surrounding culture, and even gay friends may not give us much support for staying together. Since both men are free to leave, with few economic restraints or childcare responsibilities, we need to acknowledge our own desires for a long-term relationship. We can't simply depend on a partner who has been socialized to hold us in line.[1]

Gay men in relationships handle sexual attractions in a variety of ways: some men have sex with friends or casual encounters, while still being committed to a primary partner; some men are open to having more than one lover; and others prefer sexual relations only within a monogamous relationship. The point is not to decide which approach is intrinsically better, but to figure out what really works for you and your partner. You may have some ideals about transcending jealously or fulfilling most of your needs with one man—yet your emotional reactions may not coincide with what you thought you could handle.

Much of the literature on marriage counseling assumes that "infidelity" is a function of distress between the partners. If you've agreed not to have sex outside your relationship, then a violation of your agreement without negotiating a change certainly indicates a problem in communication. But many gay men do not necessarily equate "fidelity," or a commitment to the relationship, with sexual exclusivity. Some couples openly explore sex with others while still being committed to a primary emotional relationship.

Attractions to other men don't necessarily mean you're dissatisfied with your partner. Still, it's useful to consider whether the pull toward outside sex might be a function of underlying conflicts in your relationship. You may be tempted to look elsewhere in response to problems with your lover, but you could do so at the expense of building an emotionally fulfilling relationship.

By restricting potential partners to men who feel similarly

about monogamy or open relationships, you may find some initial compatibility. Many couples, however, discover that their feelings change over time.[2] It helps to figure out how to handle this difference without immediately assuming it means the end of your relationship.[3]

Sexual versus Emotional Monogamy

An assumption often made by couples trying out nonmonogamy is that their *emotional* relationship will still be monogamous, but they're open to having other sexual encounters that don't threaten the stability of their primary relationship. Yet some men also explore the possibility of having more than one romantic involvement. This arrangement may not last long unless both of the man's partners are content with a limited relationship. While some men have more than one male lover, this dilemma is frequently faced by men who identify as bisexual.

For many gay men, bisexuality is seen as "sitting on the fence," a phase to pass through in coming out, or a way for straight men to fool around while still maintaining their "heterosexual privilege." While it may be that most men lean one way or the other, the *Kinsey Report* and other studies of sexuality have revealed a wide variation in attractions. In 1947, 37 percent of the men surveyed had had at least one sexual encounter with another man to the point of orgasm.[4] Yet we think of the general incidence of homosexuality as around 10 percent. It seems clear that many men become involved sexually with both men and women at some point in their lives.

It's helpful to look at our attractions as both emotional and sexual. We may be emotionally attracted to one person but sexually attracted to another. While it's convenient if we experience both attractions toward the same person (or the same sex), sometimes we don't. There may be different aspects about men and women you find attractive, or you may simply be attracted to a particular man or woman. Obviously, bisexuality has certain implications for your relationship, especially in terms of commitment and outside sexual partners.

If you have an open relationship, in which either partner is free to have other sexual experiences, why should having sex with a woman be any more of a threat? Conceivably, a man could have casual sex with a woman just as easily as with another man—but bisexuality seems to raise the possibility of developing a competing primary relationship. If you're considering acting on bisexual attractions (or if you're in love with more than one man), it helps to clarify whether you're really open to having more than one emotionally involved sexual relationship.

Negotiating Agreements About Outside Sex

Many gay men have unspoken agreements about sex outside their relationships, similar to the heterosexual example mentioned earlier: Joseph prefers monogamy, but to avoid an argument he doesn't say anything; while Tony enjoys sex with other partners, but keeps quiet because he assumes their relationship couldn't tolerate the disclosure. They collude with each other to ignore their difference: Joseph really doesn't want to hear about Tony's encounters, and Tony doesn't flaunt his affairs. They may peacefully coexist until Joseph comes home and finds Tony in bed with another man. This discovery precipitates a crisis, and they are forced to acknowledge their difference. Or, after the initial upheaval, they may ignore their conflict: Joseph doesn't ask any questions, and Tony tries to be more discreet.

When two men are first getting to know each other, they may hesitate to talk about outside partners because they haven't really defined their relationship. One man may think of himself as still "dating" while the other assumes they are lovers. A discussion about their expectations will help clarify this difference. Some men hesitate to define their relationship, not wanting to feel "boxed in," but part of the definition can simply be that you're not ready to identify as a couple.

Even when you've both acknowledged you're in a relationship, you needn't wait until one of you sleeps with another man in order to talk about your expectations. You can say what you want and find out how your partner feels, and then negotiate an agreement that takes you both into consideration. In the following example we'll look at how Jim and Ron sort through their feelings about sex with friends.

Jim and Ron have been together for a year. They've never discussed their assumptions about other sexual partners. Next week Ron is going to New York for a conference, and plans to stay with Keith, a former lover. In the course of their conversation, Ron imagines that he and Keith will sleep together, just for old times' sake. Jim is upset about this, and says so.

Ron tries to reassure Jim by saying "I'm not interested in getting involved with him, if that's what you're thinking."

JIM: It's not so much that; I thought we had a commitment.
RON: Sleeping with Keith seems like a violation of our commitment?
JIM: Yes, it does.
RON: I didn't mean to upset you. Why don't we talk about this, so we can come up with an agreement we both feel comfortable with.

Ron realizes they have a difference in how they view commitment and outside sexual contacts. Instead of saying "I never agreed to that," or arguing about whether sleeping with Keith violates their commitment, Ron suggests that they clarify their expectations, hoping they can find a solution that works for both of them. To deal with this problem, they decide to use the steps for resolving conflicts outlined in chapter 4.

Step 1. Clarify the Conflict

1a. Say what you'd like.

JIM: I'd rather we only had sex with each other.
RON: I'd occasionally like to sleep with friends.

1b. Distinguish desires from potential solutions. What each of them would like are really potential solutions. They first became aware of their conflict by identifying this difference, so it makes sense that they would state it this way. But what is it that "having sex only with each other" or "being able to sleep with friends" is an attempt to solve?

JIM: I want a sense that we're committed to each other. We'll work out our problems and not just go off with someone else if times get hard.

The idea at this point is to get at your *own* desires, rather than countering each other. Ron could claim that sleeping with Keith doesn't have anything to do with avoiding problems between them, but instead he simply describes what he would like.

RON: I'd like to be able to maintain close relationships with other friends, without that being a threat to our relationship.

Distinguishing desires from potential solutions can allow more room for figuring out how those desires can best be met.

Potential solutions	Underlying desires
Exclusive sexual relationship	Commitment
Sleep with friends	Close relationships with friends

By acknowledging underlying desires, a shift has occurred in how they conceptualize the conflict. This will allow them to explore what "commitment" and "closeness" really mean to *their* relationship, rather than simply arguing about monogamy versus nonmanogamy in some abstract or theoretical way.

1c. Identify behaviors and feelings; listen and reflect. The next step is to talk about what some of their experiences have been, so they can know more about each other's desires.

JIM: Rather than telling me what was wrong, my last boyfriend used our "open" relationship to find someone else.

RON [listens and reflects]: You don't trust open relationships, because Matt used nonmonogamy as a ruse to get involved with another guy.

JIM: Yeah. Supposedly it didn't mean anything that he was having sex with others, when all the while he was looking for someone else, and never said a word to me about what the problem was.

RON: You must have felt really betrayed.

JIM: I did.

RON: You're afraid that if I sleep with Keith the same thing might happen again.

JIM: Sure. If you're happy with me, why should you have to go looking for sex with anyone else? And if you're not, I want you to tell me, so we can work it out. That's what commitment means to me.

RON: I see. If something's wrong, you want to work it through, rather than going off to find someone else.

JIM: Right.

In the above exchange, Ron refrained from insisting that his friendship with Keith has nothing to do with how Jim was treated by Matt. Because he reflected Jim's feelings, Jim is more likely to listen to Ron's desire for close relationships with his friends.

RON: I'm not tempted to get something going with Keith, or anyone else. But Keith and I have always slept together whenever we've seen each other. Most of the time we don't even have sex. If we feel like it, fine, but it's not the focus of our involvement.

JIM [reflects]: You just find it comforting to sleep with old friends. It's no big deal if you have sex or not.

RON: Right. For me, *not* sleeping together puts more emphasis on sex, by making it seem as if our desire for closeness is this forbidden thing. Just because I want to be close to someone else doesn't mean there's something wrong between us.

JIM: You want to feel close to your friends without threatening our relationship.

RON: Exactly.

Now that they at least understand each other's positions, it's time to:

Step 2. Brainstorm Alternatives

At this point, they'll list various ways to meet both their desires: Jim wants a sense of commitment, and Ron wants to feel close to his friends. Not everything they mention will be an acceptable solution; this is simply a chance to generate lots of ideas they can sort through later.

Get to know each other's friends.

Set aside time to check in with each other.

Explore our own sexual relationship.

Have a commitment ritual: exchange rings, or celebrate our relationship with an anniversary party.

Spend some time alone with friends.

Massage with friends.

Sleeping with others without sex.

No sex with mutual friends.

Only totally safe sex with friends.

Can only have sex with others when you're out of town; not at home—not in *our* bed!

Only if discussed ahead of time; not during times of stress in the relationship.

Go ahead and have outside sex; just don't tell me about it.

Lie.

Three-ways.

Step 3. Examine Potential Solutions to See If They Meet Both Your Desires. Listen and Reflect

They go through the list and take turns talking about how each of these ideas would address their desires:

1. *Get to know each other's friends.*

JIM: If I got to know some of your friends, I'd feel more relaxed when you spend time with them.

RON: Seeing us together would help you feel less suspicious?

JIM: I think so.

RON: I'd like you to meet them anyway. Though I also enjoy spending time with them alone.

2. *Set aside time to check in with each other.*

RON: This sounds like a good idea to me. Lately it seems like weeks go by without us ever really talking.

JIM: It seems a little formal, but I'd be willing to try it.

3. *Explore our own sexual relationship.*

RON: Did you think I wasn't satisfied?

JIM: You tell me.

RON: It's been fine, but why not explore some new things anyway? It could be fun.

4. *Have a commitment ritual.*

RON: This seems a little artificial to me.
JIM: It reminds you of marriage?
RON: Yes. Why copy heterosexual models?
JIM: I don't want a wedding, exactly, but I'd like to find some way to celebrate with our friends.
RON: Maybe we could brainstorm some ideas for that later.
JIM: All right.

5. *Spend some time alone with friends.*

RON: We already covered this one.

6. *Massage.*

RON: What do you think of massage with friends?
JIM: I get too aroused.
RON: Does that make you uncomfortable?
JIM: I don't want them to think I'm coming on to them.
RON: Just because you get a hard-on doesn't mean you have to do anything with it.
JIM: Well, you know how one thing leads to another.
RON: Oh? Tell me about it.
JIM: I guess it's back to whether or not sex with others means a lack of commitment in our relationship.
RON: How do you feel about that now?
JIM: Still a little wary.
RON: Why don't we go through the rest of the list?
JIM: All right.

7. *Sleeping with others without sex.*

JIM: Be serious.
RON: You and I do that all the time. Well, not all the time. Anyway, it's possible.

JIM: You think it's just cozy, is that it?

RON: For the most part. Like I said, if something comes up, it's not that big a deal.

JIM: Like having a wet dream.

RON: Something like that.

JIM: Let's move on.

8. *No sex with mutual friends.*

RON: This one seems to contradict your desire to get to know my friends.

JIM: That's right—if I get to know them, then you can't sleep with them anymore. [Jim nudges Ron.]

RON: Let's move on, wise guy.

9. *Only totally safe sex with friends.*

JIM: Definitely none of this "possibly safe" sex.

RON: So it's all right to have sex as long as it's safe?

JIM: Not so fast. I'm just saying *if* we decide it's all right, it has to be totally safe.

RON: That sounds fine to me.

10. *Can only have sex with others when you're out of town; not at home—not in* our *bed.*

RON: What about friends visiting from out of town?

JIM: So where would I be?

RON: How about three-ways?

JIM: You're skipping ahead.

RON: If you tolerate this at all, it's only if you're not available, is that it?

JIM: Right. You said you weren't looking for another relationship.

RON: That's true. Next.

11. *Only if discussed ahead of time; not during times of stress in the relationship.*

RON: No spontaneous encounters?

JIM: If you're going off to New York to stay with Keith, I don't want to find out you've met some model from Amsterdam you just happened to feel "cozy" with.

RON: So you want to limit it to friends.

JIM: Yes. I want to know where you are.

RON: This second part seems important: not during times of stress. Would that help you feel more secure about our commitment?

JIM: If you had sex with someone when we were having a hard time, I'd figure you were trying to find someone else.

RON: I see.

12. *Go ahead and have outside sex; just don't tell me about it.*

JIM: When I don't know, I imagine all sorts of things. I'd rather know.

RON: I'd like to know, too.

13. *Lie.*

JIM: Same as above.

14. *Three-ways.*

JIM: I don't know about that.

RON: It could be fun.

JIM: I'd feel left out.

RON: We could make sure you don't.

JIM: It just doesn't appeal to me.

RON: Not even with Ben?

JIM: Oh, stop.

RON: Well, think about it.

JIM: Not even for a second.

After going through this list, they may want to summarize what they feel comfortable with at this point. Since Ron is going to New York next week, they decide to concentrate on an agreement that would apply to this trip.

* * *

Step 4. Select a Tentative Solution

RON: What would you feel comfortable with?

JIM: I'd feel all right if you just slept together. I guess for right now I'd still rather you didn't have sex.

RON: It seems like you're feeling pretty vulnerable.

JIM: I understand you want to be close to your friends, but I don't want anything to come between us. Maybe I need some reassurance for a while.

RON: Sex with friends is still something I'm interested in, but I'm willing to put it off for now. So what do you say we "explore" a little sex ourselves?

JIM: I don't know, what if something came up?

RON: I think we could handle it.

Step 5. Try Out the Solution for a Trial Run

Ron goes to New York and tells Keith about their agreement. Keith gives him a hard time, and Ron feels irritated with both of them. During the night, Ron has trouble falling asleep. He starts to masturbate, hoping an orgasm will relax him. Keith notices, and reaches over to help him out. Ron remembers his promise, but figures what's the difference.

At home, Jim imagines Ron sleeping with Keith, and feels very anxious.

Step 6. Set Aside Time to Evaluate How It's Working

Ron comes home, and they avoid the subject for a few days. Jim doesn't want to seem jealous, and expects Ron to tell him what happened. Ron has no intention of bringing it up, hoping the entire issue will simply go away. The effort it takes to avoid this discussion leaves them both feeling rather tense.

One night over dinner, Jim says, "You haven't said much about your trip."

RON: It went all right. [Silence.]

JIM: How was Keith?

RON: Doing okay. He started a new job in the Village.

JIM [taking a deep breath]: So how did he react?

RON: React to what?

JIM: Ron, I'm tired of pulling teeth.

RON: He gave me a hard time, and I got pissed off.

JIM: At him, or at me?

RON: Both.

JIM: He should have been more understanding.

RON: Yeah, well, he wasn't.

JIM: Well, thank you anyway for standing up to him. Are you still mad at me?

RON: I don't know.

JIM: You don't know?

RON: No, I guess not.

JIM: You are, I can tell.

RON: I'm not mad at you, all right?

JIM: You sound pissed off.

RON: All right, I'm still irritated. I don't see what difference it makes whether you jerk yourself off or someone else does it for you.

JIM [staring at Ron]: Are you telling me—[Ron averts his eyes, and looks out the window.] I don't believe this.

RON [trying to head him off]: It's not what you think—

JIM: I thought I could trust you.

RON: Well, you can; it's just—

JIM: This is exactly what I was afraid of.

RON: Look, don't get carried away—

JIM: You said you wouldn't have sex, and you did!

RON: It wasn't like we really made love—

JIM: What do you call it, then?

RON: It was nothing. We were—

JIM: Nothing! A promise means nothing to you?

RON: It wasn't like that. If you would just listen—

JIM: Listen to a pack of lies!

RON: You're obviously upset—

JIM: Upset? Why should I be upset? My lover has sleazy sex with some slut from New York, after lying through his teeth—

RON: You're getting hysterical and you don't even know what happened.

JIM: You lied to me! You said you wouldn't have sex and you did.

RON: Look, I told him I didn't want to have sex, all right?

JIM: So did he rape you, or what?

RON: Not exactly. But I couldn't sleep, and thought if I jerked off—

JIM: I don't want to hear this.

RON: Well, he noticed, and sort of . . . helped out. That's all. It wasn't like we made love or anything.

JIM: What's a little orgasm between friends.

RON: You're not being fair.

JIM: Don't talk to me about fair!

RON: Listen, it wasn't that easy for me, either.

JIM: No, I bet it was really *hard.*

RON: Do you want to work this out or not?

JIM: You broke your promise!

RON: Well, it was a goddamn stupid promise!

JIM: You don't even care about my feelings—

RON: I never should have told you. It was nothing!

We might expect Jim to go on at some length about his sense of betrayal, and Ron to defend himself. It's probably unrealistic to expect them to step back and reflect each other's feelings, because they're both so upset. They might call each other names, retaliate with sarcasm, and threaten to end the relationship in order to demonstrate their pain. So long as neither of them feels acknowledged, they tend to repeat themselves: Jim feels betrayed, and Ron claims it was no big deal. After a while, they may go through this enough times for one of them to back off and listen.

RON: Okay, I broke our agreement. I understand you feel hurt.

JIM: If you understood, then why did you do it?

RON: You really feel betrayed. [He sidesteps the temptation to explain himself again, and stays with what he imagines Jim is feeling.]

JIM: Of course I feel betrayed.

RON: It's hard to trust me right now.

JIM: How can I trust you?

RON: You feel really hurt.

JIM: I do feel hurt. I don't know what you want, or whether you really care for me—

RON: I do care for you—

JIM: That's a fine way to show it.

Ron is silent for a moment. Jim is hostile because he feels hurt, but he also cares for Ron and fears their relationship is threatened. Recognizing the positive intent behind Jim's sarcasm helps Ron avoid retaliating. Instead, he comments on their process.

RON: You feel hurt and I'm being defensive. Why don't we back off and see if we can take turns just trying to understand each other.

Jim grudgingly agrees, not sure he's ready to back off, since he still feels betrayed.

RON: You're obviously disappointed and angry with me.
JIM: Yes I am. You made a promise and you betrayed me.
RON: Breaking my promise seems even more of an issue than sleeping with Keith.
JIM: I already said it was all right to sleep together, but that wasn't enough, was it.
RON: You're afraid I'm really not interested in you. [He ignores Jim's bait.]

Because Ron is making an effort to understand how Jim was affected, Jim is able to go more deeply into his feelings:

JIM: After you left, I realized I wasn't ready to handle outside relationships. When you came home, you were so cold and distant, I knew something had happened.
RON: You thought I was going to dump you.
JIM: It really scares me to think we could let what we have slip through our fingers. [Ron is quiet, but touches Jim's hand.]
JIM [crying]: I don't want to lose you.
RON: [puts his arm around Jim, and draws him close]: I don't want to lose you, either.

He strokes Jim's hair while Jim sobs against his chest. Tears come to his eyes, too, and they're quiet as they hold each other.

After a while, Jim sits up and reaches for a tissue. He blows his nose and says, "What about you?"

RON: When Keith gave me a hard time, I was irritated with him for not respecting our agreement, and I was pissed at you for not trusting me.

JIM [nods]: You must have been fed up with both of us.

RON: I was also mad at myself for agreeing to something I didn't really believe in. I felt horny and couldn't sleep, so I decided to jerk off. Then when Keith grabbed me, I thought what the hell. I understand you got burned by Matt. But I know myself; I'm not worried about trying to find someone else.

JIM: You wish I'd stop thinking you're going to leave me.

RON: Right. I'm trying to take your feelings into consideration, but I want you to appreciate where I'm coming from—I'm not being irresponsible just because I want to feel close to other friends.

JIM: You'd like to sleep with your friends without threatening our relationship.

RON: I really would.

JIM: If it helps any, I *wish* I could handle it, but I felt miserable while you were gone. Having sex with others is not okay with me, and I'm not going to pretend everything's fine.

RON: Well, so what should we do?

At this point, they realize they've reached an impasse. If none of their solutions satisfies both of them, what options do they have now? Are they willing to give up their relationship, hoping to find someone else who might be more compatible? They may be, in which case they can recognize their difference with some regret, but also acknowledge that the gulf that separates them is insurmountable. Rather than leaping immediately to this conclusion, they decide to take a break.

Step 3: Examine Potential Solutions to See If They Meet Both of Your Desires. If None Do:

3a. Take a break. They spend some time by themselves to sort through their feelings and examine what this difference really means to them.

3b. Shift from the context of the conflict to the value of the relationship. On their own, they shift from the dispute about outside sexual partners to how much they value their relationship.

Jim thinks about what they could build together in the future. He remembers how miserable he felt the previous week, knowing Ron was with Keith. But then he imagines sleeping alone, not being with Ron at all, starting all over trying to find someone else—or giving up, and just being by himself for a while.

Ron also wrestles with what the relationship means to him. He's annoyed with Jim's insecurity about sex with friends, even though he understands why he feels that way.

They both really love each other. They don't want to split up. But it's hard for Jim to understand how Ron could give up what they have in order to satisfy some casual indulgence; likewise, Ron doesn't understand why Jim feels so threatened by his closeness to other friends.

They'd each like the other to change. But you can't really change anyone else—you can only change yourself. So they move on to the next step.

3c. Think about what you could offer to resolve the impasse. Ron thinks maybe he's being too stubborn; after all, he hadn't had sex with anyone for months before he met Jim. It's not as if he has the hots for every man who walks down the street. But when he slept with Keith, refraining from sex made it seem all the more attractive, just because it was forbidden. He knows they shouldn't have gotten it on—or else he should never have promised not to. But why is any of this such a big deal? They're just friends.

On the other hand, is sex really the issue? He's willing to be influenced by Jim's concerns, but he doesn't want to feel controlled by the hurt from Jim's previous relationship. He imagines losing Jim simply to maintain his option of being able to sleep occasionally with friends. What could he offer? At least for the time being, not to have sex with anyone else and to work on building the level of trust in their relationship.

Meanwhile, Jim recognizes that Ron isn't Matt, but wishing his fears would simply go away doesn't seem to change them. Maybe Jim could possibly tolerate some anxiety in order to gain more trust in their relationship, rather than trying to totally control what Ron does.

3d. *Come back and say what you're willing to offer.*

RON: I'm sure I could handle outside partners without threatening our relationship, but I realize you feel strongly about this. Being with you is more important to me than sleeping with other friends. So I'm willing to put this off for now, while we build some trust in our relationship.

JIM: It really helps to hear that. Part of my insecurity comes from not knowing whether I'm really important to you. I think I could live with your desire to be sexual with others at some point if we made some agreements about safe sex and acknowledged our commitment.

Ron feels released from such an intense desire to have sex with others, simply because Jim has recognized his independence. Jim feels more relaxed because Ron has acknowledged how much he means to him. They decide to put off negotiations about sleeping with others for a few months while they develop some trust in their relationship.

Working Through

Every couple needs to figure out how they want to deal with outside sex, independence, and commitment. The above example shows how conflicts about monogamy may be a function of other issues in your relationship. If you get to what's really at the core of your feelings toward each other, this can allow movement in what might originally have felt like irreconcilable differences.

You may both decide that an exclusive relationship (or an open one) is what you want when you first get together. But when you stop having outside sex (or you try sleeping with other men), you can't always predict how you're going to react, no matter what you've rationally attempted to negotiate. Sometimes our ideals don't match how we really feel. You may need to adjust your ideals to what you can both handle emotionally.

Shifting from the particular *content* (such as monogamy versus nonmonogamy) to the *process* of what's going on between you (affirming your desires for independence and commitment) can help you understand the function of similar conflicts in your relationship. By negotiating underlying desires, you're less likely to reach an impasse over the first solution that occurs to you.

You're unlikely to always get what you want in your relationship. However, staying together may be more important to you than having your way about a particular issue. Working through these conflicts can strengthen your relationship by helping you clarify what you really want from each other. You learn how to meet your own desires while still taking your partner's feelings into consideration.

Questions and Comments

Q: My lover had sex with another guy despite our agreement to be monogamous, and now it's hard for me to trust him.

A: Discussing this violation can help you both make sense of his behavior—was it a move on his part to express dissatisfaction, assert his independence, or reassure himself of his attractiveness? Does he see it as a slip, or does he want to renegotiate your agreement about monogamy?

Trust in a relationship doesn't have to be all or nothing. Does he continue to be trustworthy in other ways? Sometimes couples break up prematurely to dramatize their hurt. Give yourselves some time to sort through your feelings and figure out what this means for your relationship.

Q: My boyfriend is constantly suspicious I'm getting it on with other guys. I can never reassure him enough, and it's making me question our relationship.

A: His fear that he may lose you has the danger of becoming a self-fulfilling prophecy. Couples therapy could provide a safe place for him to say more about his feelings of insecurity, and for you to let him know how you're affected by his fears. A neutral mediator can help de-escalate the spiral of suspicion and reaction that has developed between you.

Q: Three years ago I slept with my lover's best friend, and I still haven't heard the end of it. I don't get any credit for the last three years, and frankly I wonder why I'm bothering anymore.

A: The obvious problem with dredging up incidents from the past is that it rekindles previous arguments and distracts from the current conflict. Rather than getting into another argument over past transgressions, it might be helpful to use this issue as a signal for feelings in the present: "You're bringing up my affair with Jason again; I wonder if you're annoyed with me." Then you can work on what's upsetting him now.

9

Family Matters

*T*he relatively recent development of the nuclear family (consisting of a wife, husband, and two kids) has been eclipsed by a wealth of diversity. Families today take the form of single parents, unmarried partners, multiple generations, and our own gay and lesbian families.

In this chapter we'll explore various ways we can include one another in our emerging sense of family: coming out to our parents and siblings; dealing with conflict over the "in-laws"; involvement with children; and seeing our friends as family.

Coming Out to Parents

Coming out to our families is a significant event for most gay men. We may have thought about disclosing our sexual orientation for a long time, hoping our parents would appreciate our desire to include them in our lives. Revealing such an intimate aspect of ourselves is an attempt to let our families know who we really are, so our future relationships can be more genuine.

But a sense of renewed openness in a family can take a while, if it happens at all. Some parents are very disappointed, especially in the beginning. Disclosing your sexual orientation and dealing with the emotional fallout can be an arduous process.

The following ideas can help you take care of yourself and still keep the lines of communication open with your family, even if they're upset by your revelation.

Guidelines for Coming Out

There's some pressure in the gay community to come out as a political act—the more of us who do, the easier it will be for everyone. At the same time, it's important to balance this potential social benefit with how you imagine it will affect your relationship with your family. Everyone's situation is unique: you need to decide whether you want to tell your parents you're gay, and think about how you'd like to tell them (in person, by letter, or by phone) and what you'd like to communicate to them about what this means to you.

Come Out When You're Feeling Good About Yourself

Some men reach out to their families for understanding and support when they're feeling emotionally vulnerable. However, your parents may have such a deep emotional response to your disclosure that they won't be able to help you sort through your feelings. Sensing your uncertainty, they may also reinforce your confusion. It helps to have already worked through most of your own doubts about your sexual orientation before you tell your parents.

Have a Support System

It's vital to have some supportive friends who can help you deal with your own feelings of disappointment or relief after you've told your parents. Your support system may include your lover, other gay friends, a counselor, a brother or sister you've told before—anyone you feel close to who will be available before, during, and after your disclosure.

Tell your partner about your plans and what you hope to gain by coming out. Say how you think your parents will react, and imagine how you'll feel if they respond with hostility or refuse to discuss it. You can expect a lot of feelings to surface when you talk to your parents—not just in them, but in you, especially in response to their reaction. Above all, *don't* tell your parents you're gay when you're feeling alone and have no one else to talk to.

Listen and Reflect

You've had time to think about this and you've prepared how you want to tell them, but they're hearing this for the first time, so it's up to you to step back and listen to them. At this point you don't need to counter their objections or educate them about their prejudices. Just listen to how it feels for them to hear this news. They may be so focused on their own hurt that it's difficult for them to communicate their caring for you, but you may be able to recognize the concern underlying their disappointment.

They will need to go through their own process of coming out (at least to themselves) as parents of a gay son. They'll probably have the same doubts, denial, and fears of recrimination that you had yourself. After the initial shock, they may realize you're still the same person and be willing to reexamine their assumptions about what this means for your future.

Limit Your Interaction

It's best not to turn your disclosure into a marathon—both you and your family will have many reactions that will take a while to sort through. You're probably not the best person to help them process their feelings. After you've reflected their concerns and affirmed your desire for continued contact, they may be willing to reach out to Parents and Friends of Lesbians and Gays for support from other parents.[1]

If their initial response is hostile, you can try to empathize with their reaction, but you needn't subject yourself to threats, disparaging comments, or verbal abuse. Call a time-out, and let them know you'll contact them later, once you've all had a chance to cool off.

Don't Retaliate

Far from appreciating how difficult it must have been for you to reveal such an intimate part of yourself, they may take out their disappointment on you. If you can simply hear that they're upset and avoid retaliating, you may be able to keep the conflict from escalating. You can recognize that your parents are hurting, no doubt because of the prejudices they were brought up with; they need to grieve for the loss of who they imagined you were. We may have taken years to come to terms with our sexual orientation, so it's no surprise that our families will take a while to adjust to this information.

You've revealed something very intimate about yourself, hoping to feel closer to your family. If they respond negatively, you'll probably feel hurt and angry. Tell your friends how you feel, and give yourself time to sort through what you'd like to communicate to your family. Not everything has to be resolved at once.

Keep Channels of Communication Open

You may need some time apart following your initial disclosure. But some families cut off communications to demonstrate their hurt, and set unrealistic conditions for future contact, which makes it difficult to reach out again later. Don't assume that ultimatums made in the heat of retaliation must last forever. Do your part to keep communications open—write or telephone when you feel calmer yourself. Listen to them and reflect their feelings—acknowledge their disappointment and underlying concern. Let them know that the reason you decided to tell them was that you wanted to feel closer, and stress your desire for continued contact.

Stages of Acceptance

We all come to terms with significant changes at our own pace. Just as we take varying lengths of time to come out ourselves, so parents go through their own process of absorbing this news. As much as we'd like them to appreciate our willingness to reveal such an intimate part of ourselves, it's unlikely that they'll be able to skip ahead to acceptance without going through some of the following stages first.

Disbelief

It's amazing how strong some parents' denial is, even when it's pretty obvious we're not meeting the usual time line for heterosexual involvements. Many parents don't think of their children as being sexual at all, much less homosexual. Even if they suspected it in the back of their minds, most parents are shocked to find out we're gay.

Tell Me It Isn't So

They may think you're rebelling, you're going through a phase, or you were seduced by your lover. The possibility that you're simply in touch with your own feelings may be beyond their comprehension. They may plead with you to tell them you're not really gay. It's beginning to sink in; their sorrow and childlike wishful thinking are a natural part of their own process of grieving for the loss of who they thought you were.

Rejection

Many parents see our disclosure as a personal affront. They think we chose to be gay (or to come out) purposefully to hurt them, rather than seeing that we're actually trying to be closer to them by telling them who we really are.

They finally see that you're quite serious about this "madness." Feeling overwhelmed, they may attempt to counter your disclosure by demanding that you forsake being gay. What you feel is not important; they claim you owe it to your family not to throw your life away and humiliate them. Because of their own feelings of being out of control, they may try to overpower you with threats to withdraw financial or emotional support.

Let's Pretend

You refuse to go back into the closet, but you also don't escalate the conflict with your own ultimatums that they accept you or forget you. You reach an uneasy coexistence—they'll tolerate your being around, but they don't really want to hear about your sexual orientation. You're not sure whether to keep trying to get through to them, or if you should edit half of your existence from conversation, just so they won't get upset. You may not get much support from telling them about your life anyway, so after a while you stop trying. Your family acts as if you'd never said anything, and you begin to wonder whether you're invisible.

A Shift Occurs

Something changes—you get a lover or lose one; you have a child, or there's an illness in the family. A new stress on the system causes a shift in your family's dynamics. Suddenly you or your parents see each other differently—your father cherishes your baby; your mother gets to know your lover; your sister reaches out to you when her husband dies. A new perspective about what's really important allows you to come together again.

Acceptance

Some families are able to accommodate your disclosure without needing a crisis to remind them of your importance to one another. After an initial negative reaction, many families are able to affirm their continuing love and support—they see that you're still you, even if they have concerns about how your life will be affected. Some parents move beyond merely accepting the fact their son is gay: they genuinely appreciate the caring behind your disclosure and your desire to include them.[2]

And If Nothing Seems to Work?

Despite their attempts to reach out, some gay men become alienated from their families. Their parents refuse to talk to them, read about homosexuality, or discuss it with even their closest friends. They bury their grief, and their resentment smolders. Some of us are cut off altogether, and verbally (or even physically) abused when we make contact. If this happens with your family, you can remain open to the possibility that someday the situation could change, without blaming yourself for the estrangement.

Though you wish you could enable them to feel better about your homosexuality, you really have no control over how anyone feels about you. You can learn some skills to make it less likely that conflicts will escalate, but you're not responsible for their reactions. It's up to both sides to make it work—they have to want continued contact, as well as you.

It's hard to tell what might develop eventually. Seeing that we're content, that we're respectful of other people and caring in our relationships, some parents who reject us initially find ways to accommodate our lifestyle, perhaps more by our example than from our attempts to convince them of anything. You may be able to maintain some kind of relationship, even if it never quite fits what either of you had hoped for.

*   *   *

Recognizing Our Relationships

Married couples often experience stress in dealing with the in-laws, but parents usually acknowledge the marriage and accept one's spouse as part of the family (for better or worse). Families help buffer conflicts within the couple by taking the marriage seriously, giving financial assistance, and providing emotional support. But many parents have a hard time extending this same acknowledgment to gay relationships.

When we're not involved with anyone, our families may still hold on to the illusion that one day we'll meet the right woman and everything will be fine. When we become involved in a long-term relationship with another man, it's harder for them to pretend that our sexual orientation is just a phase. Your parents may be willing to tolerate the fact that you're gay without being ready to meet your partner, much less include him in family gatherings. They may wonder why you have to make such an issue about your orientation by "flaunting" it in everyone's face, not recognizing how heterosexuality permeates every aspect of their world.

Strains can develop between you and your partner when your family pretends he doesn't exist, or denies the significance of your relationship. In the following example we'll look at how Alex and Jeff handle an invitation to the wedding of Alex's sister.

Alex comes from a middle-class black family, and was recently invited to his sister's wedding. Though his parents know he's gay, Jeff has never been invited to family gatherings, and wasn't included this time either. Alex has never forced the issue. Jeff, however, has invited Alex to meet his family, and they've even slept together at his parents' house. He has a hard time understanding why Alex isn't willing to confront his family.

Jeff could interpret Alex's reluctance as a sign of internalized homophobia, or as an indication that he doesn't really take their relationship seriously. Alex could experience Jeff's insistence on a showdown as insensitive. Interpretations tend to undermine the mutual support they could both use when dealing with their families. Instead, they say how they feel, and try to understand each other's position.

JEFF: I feel invisible to your family, and I wonder whether I'm really important to you.

Rather than immediately answering him, Alex reflects Jeff's concerns.

ALEX: You feel left out, and wish I'd stand up to my family?

JEFF: Yes. Your brother wouldn't go if his wife wasn't invited. Your family's not recognizing our relationship.

Alex then says more about how the situation affects him:

ALEX: Of course you're important to me. It's hard on me when my family ignores you, but Lucy's wedding is a major family event, and I want to be there for my sister.

JEFF [reflects Alex's feelings]: You care for me, but you also want to attend your sister's wedding.

ALEX: I'd like my parents to recognize our relationship too, but they think I'm throwing my life away.

JEFF: Do you feel pressured to choose between me and your family?

ALEX: I don't care any less for you just because I'm trying to get along with my parents and I want to celebrate my sister's wedding.

JEFF: I took a risk with my parents when I brought you home. I wonder why you're not as willing to challenge yours.

ALEX: I'm glad you've introduced me to your parents. But I wonder whether you appreciate the risks I've already taken by coming out to my family.

Gay men from various ethnic groups may feel torn between their loyalty to their ethnic identification and their identity as gay men. Their own community may reject them, while at the same time they have to contend with racism in the gay white subculture.

In many ethnic communities there is less emphasis on the individual's personal fulfillment and more consideration for what's good for the family. Alex may not feel that he's in a position to make the same demands on his family that Jeff is willing to make on his. It's not very pleasant to think that you have to choose between your lover and your family. To approach this dilemma, they try to distinguish potential solutions from underlying desires.

Potential solution

Bring Jeff to the wedding

Underlying desires

Affirm relationship
Maintain contact with family

Shifting from the potential *solution* (whether to bring Jeff to the wedding) helps them consider other possibilities for meeting their underlying desires. They could go on to brainstorm, and come up with various ways to acknowledge their relationship and also maintain Alex's relationship with his family. Whatever they decide about the wedding, they can use this conflict to clarify their expectations about family contact, respect their differences, and affirm their caring for each other.

Having a Child

In the last few years many gay men have become parents through adoption, foster care, and coparenting arrangements with lesbians. The preparation, planning, and level of agreement that are necessary to have kids requires us to think about this commitment very thoroughly. In the following example we'll see how Sam and Rob sort through their conflict over having children.

Sam has always wanted to have a child. Rob likes kids, but he doesn't want to be a parent. Without immediately assuming they're incompatible, they decide to go through the steps for resolving conflicts in order to discover whether there's a way to resolve this difference.

Step 1: Clarify the Conflict

1a. Say what you'd like.

SAM: I'd like to have a kid.
ROB: I'd rather not have kids.

1b. Distinguish desires from potential solutions. Sam wants a child in his life but he's not sure how—whether he wants to adopt one, have a child with a woman friend, or some other arrangement. Rob doesn't want primary responsibility for a child, and is unsure about more peripheral involvement.

They both affirm their desire to stay together as a couple, and go on to outline their underlying desires.

Potential solution	*Underlying desires*
Have a kid versus not having a kid	Parenting a child Not having primary responsibility Maintain relationship

1c. Identify behaviors and feelings; listen and reflect.
They don't have a child yet, so they say more about each of their desires.

SAM: I'm ready for the day-to-day involvement and responsibility of caring for a child, but I wonder how I can include you if you're not interested.

ROB: I'm also concerned whether there would still be room for me if you had a kid.

They go on to brainstorm to see if there's some way to accommodate their desires.

Step 2. Brainstorm Alternatives

They come up with the following list:

Sam could coparent with a lesbian couple.

We could have separate apartments.

Sam could be a parent, and Rob wouldn't be expected to be involved with the child.

Sam could live with a coparent, and Rob could visit.

Sam could be an "uncle" to the child of another gay or lesbian couple, and we could still live together.

Step 3. Examine Potential Solutions to See If They Meet Both Your Desires

They talk about what these solutions would be like for them.

SAM: When you say you don't want to be a parent, does that mean you don't want to live with a kid, either?

ROB: Even if I don't see myself as a parent, I think whoever is in the home seems like a parent to the child.

SAM: I'd want a coparent, preferably in my own home.

ROB: You feel really strongly about coparenting, don't you?

SAM: Yes. If you're not interested in being involved with the child, I'd still want someone to coparent with me. But that doesn't mean I'm looking for another lover.

Step 4. Select a Tentative Solution

At this point Sam will explore coparenting options with some lesbian friends. Another set of agreements would need to be worked out with them, and this in turn would affect his relationship with Rob. It's important that they keep in touch about how their plans are developing and how they affect their own relationship.

If none of their brainstorming ideas satisfied them, they could take a break and shift from the content of the conflict to valuing their relationship. Is having a child, or not living with a child, more important than maintaining their relationship? If Sam wants a coparent who is also his lover, or if Rob wants a partner who isn't distracted by the needs of a child, they may not be able to work something out. Identifying their underlying desires will allow them to explore various options: perhaps Sam could coparent with another friend, for example, but still maintain his relationship with Rob.

Coparenting Agreements

When you decide to coparent, it's important to be very clear about your expectations.[3] It helps to draw up an agreement about the nature of your relationship, both with your own partner and with the child's mother (and partner): will you be coparenting the child equally? Or will you be more of an "uncle" to the child, without parenting rights or responsibilities? Depending on your level of involvement, you'll need to decide whose names will appear on the birth certificate, how expenses will be divided, and how much time you'll have with the child.

While no one likes to focus on potential disputes in the midst of your excitement about bringing a new child into the world, it's important to determine a method for resolving disagreements. Possibilities include mediations with friends or hiring a professional counselor to help you sort through your conflicts.

You can use the listening and negotiating skills you've learned to make sure you both feel heard and understood. In order for an agreement about coparenting to work in the interests of your child, you both need to feel confident you'll be part of these decisions.

Custody Disputes

Many people don't realize their sexual orientation until after they've married and had children. While not all marriages necessarily end just because one partner is gay, sexual orientation may become an issue in a custody dispute. Divorce can be very painful, and a battle over custody may have more to do with retribution than with determining the best interests of the children. By acknowledging each other's disappointment and fears, you may be able to separate the real custody issues and reach a satisfactory settlement through family court mediation.

Sometimes a custody battle is unavoidable, but it's important to remember that you'll both be the child's parents forever. Though older children may have some say about which parent they prefer to live with, it's important not to put your child in the position of having to choose between you emotionally. To reject either parent is an untenable choice for a child. Children often feel responsible and guilty about divorce, assuming it would never have happened if they hadn't been "bad" or had destructive fantasies. You can anticipate these reactions and reassure your children that they had nothing to do with your decision to divorce.

Coming Out to Children

Children who have grown up in an openly gay family may not be aware of any particular time their parents came out—it's as if they always knew. But they may not be very clear about what any of this means. Your own sexual relations are a private matter, but you can openly discuss what sexuality is all about, gay or straight—and encourage your children to be in touch with their own emerging sexual feelings and ask questions.

Teenagers frequently encounter the same prejudices about homosexuality in school that we did, although at least they've heard about it in the media. A sudden revelation that a parent is gay can take a while to adjust to. They may be concerned that they might "turn gay" as well; they may resent having been told, or wish they'd been told sooner. "How could I have a gay father, and how is this going to reflect on me?" is a likely reaction, even if they don't verbalize it. Though they may be surprised by this disclosure, some of the tension they felt between their parents begins to make sense.

They may have lots of questions, or may not want to discuss it at all. One day it will seem as if it doesn't make any difference, and another time they'll be acutely embarrassed to have a friend find out you're gay. Sometimes they'll be ferociously loyal, and other times admit to wishing they'd come from a "normal" family. If they live with you, they may miss their mother and resent your partner.

You can acknowledge that sometimes it's hard to come from a gay family because of society's misconceptions. Empathizing with their ambivalence will help assuage the guilt that's aroused by such contradictory feelings. When you listen to their doubts and concerns without getting defensive, they'll eventually come to terms with your disclosure at their own pace.[4]

Expanding Beyond the Relationship

When we first get involved with someone, the relationship itself becomes a focus of much of our interactions. Eventually, a desire for meaningful work, other friends, and a sense of community greater than ourselves may reemerge, and this can feel somewhat threatening.

In the past, relationships had a social function: family life served as a link to the rest of the community, and was in turn nurtured and supported by common rituals and rites of passage, such as marriage, having kids, and funerals. As our mobility has increased, this pattern has altered even for heterosexual couples, and most desires for social support have been focused on the nuclear family. This has become a weight that is difficult to bear, as evidenced by the increasing incidence of divorce, domestic violence, and child abuse.

There are a lot of stresses on gay relationships, not the least of which is a lack of recognition from the surrounding culture.

Faced with the prospect of intense discrimination, gay couples can feel extremely isolated and turn to the relationship to satisfy all of their desires for honest human contact. Unless we develop our own sense of community, we can burden our relationships with unrealistic expectations of what they are likely to provide for us.[5]

Friends as Family

The notion of "family" for gay men and lesbians may transcend parents, siblings, and other relatives. Family for us may include partners, children, former lovers, other couples, and close friends. Friendships provide stimulation and bring out other dynamics in your relationship. A shared history of struggle and mutual support fosters a sense of involvement and caring that continues over the years—we nurture one another, listen to one another's sorrows and fears, celebrate together, and make plans for the future.

Sometimes it's difficult to figure out how to relate as a couple to single friends. Many heterosexual partners object to their spouse's having friendships with the opposite sex. With gay men, our confidant, best friend, and former boyfriend (or potential lover!) might all be the same person. It helps to figure out how to have private time with friends, without threatening your relationship.

When you first become involved with someone, your friends may end up doing most of the initiating. If you decide not to go out, you're still together, so it may not occur to you to reach out to single friends. You may disappear into your relationship for months on end, forgetting that friendships need nurturing too.

We can develop new ways to include each other in our lives. Sometimes it's not easy to reach out, because of the pain and isolation we've felt in the past. It may be hard to trust that our new bonds will last, or ever replace what we hoped we might have had with our families of origin. It takes some work, but many of us are open to forging supportive ties that endure throughout our lives.

Questions and Comments

Q: My parents made it clear they didn't want to discuss my homosexuality years ago, when I first came out. At the time I didn't want to argue about it anymore either. Now I have a lover, and I'd like to include him in family gatherings.

A: It's hard to renegotiate the agreement "Let's not talk about it" without bringing it up (and thereby violating your implicit understanding). You can let them know you'd like to broach a topic that you realize they have strong feelings about, and see whether they're willing to discuss it. If not, you may want to explore how to include your partner with other family members who are more receptive.

Q: I fathered a child with a woman I met in a coparenting group, with the understanding that we'd be parenting the child together. Now she and her lover say they've changed their minds; they're willing to let me do "childcare" once in a while, but they no longer consider me an equal partner. What can I do about this?

A: Coparenting contracts between lesbians and gay men are recent developments, largely untested in courts of law. Important as it is to work out agreements beforehand, they're dependent to a large extent on the goodwill of both parties. Ask them to meet with you and a mediator to see if you can find some acceptable middle ground. If they refuse, contact an attorney familiar with family law to see what your next step should be.[6]

10

When a Lover Has AIDS

*A*t no other time has our ability to pull together as a community been tested so severely as in response to the AIDS epidemic. Far from allowing this crisis to divide us, we've provided one another with both emotional and practical support. Gay men, lesbians, and people with AIDS have lobbied for funding, pressed for an acceleration of drug testing, sensitized the medical profession, volunteered for research studies, and countered AIDS-related discrimination. We've developed a model for education that other communities at risk have adopted to combat the spread of this syndrome.

In this chapter we'll look at the continuum of AIDS infection, common responses to life-threatening illness, and how you can provide support and handle conflicts when you or your partner is infected by HIV (the AIDS virus).

HIV Infection

The continuum of infection includes being positive for the antibody to the AIDS virus; developing AIDS-related condition (or ARC); and being diagnosed with Acquired Immune Deficiency Syndrome (AIDS).

Positive Antibody Test

This test indicates whether you have developed antibodies to HIV. A positive result means you've been infected with the AIDS virus. You may feel fine, and show few signs of anything wrong with your immune system, apart from a low T-cell count. (See chapter 7 for a discussion of guidelines for antibody testing.)

AIDS-Related Condition (ARC)

This condition includes symptoms such as night sweats, swollen lymph nodes, or candida (a yeast infection). For a diagnosis of ARC, these symptoms must persist for an extended period of time and not be explainable by another illness.

Acquired Immune Deficiency Syndrome (AIDS)

AIDS is confirmed by the diagnosis of an opportunistic infection, such as Kaposi's sarcoma or pneumocystis pneumonia. These diseases are called "opportunistic" because people don't contract them unless their immune system has been damaged.

At the present time, we don't know exactly what testing positive for the HIV antibody means for the future, or whether everyone with ARC will come down with AIDS. A few people with AIDS have survived for a number of years, while others have died soon after being diagnosed. Many people in all three categories maintain their health for extended periods of time. This uncertainty over one's prognosis is very stressful, and contributes to a wide range of coping strategies.

Response to Life-Threatening Illness

Kübler-Ross identifies five stages that people often experience in response to life-threatening illness, which can help us understand a loved one's reaction to HIV infection:[1]

1. Denial (or what may be seen as "selective attention")
2. Bargaining
3. Depression
4. Anger
5. Acceptance

It's important to see these reactions as *descriptive* of how people often respond, and not as a *prescription* for what you're supposed to experience at any particular moment. But it can be reassuring to know that others have similar feelings and you're not alone in your response. With this in mind, let's look at these stages and see how they fit your own experience.

1. Denial, or Selective Attention

The concept of denial describes the difficulty we have comprehending the implications of life-threatening illness and imagining nonexistence. Though many men suspect they've been infected with HIV for a long time, it can still be quite a shock to have this confirmed through a positive antibody test or the diagnosis of an opportunistic infection. Denial refers to the sense of unreality that many people experience when they receive this news. Some people respond with sorrow, and reach out to others immediately. But you may feel numb, as though nothing has really happened. You think you should be feeling more than you actually are, but the enormity of this revelation hasn't really sunk in.

The word "denial" has a negative connotation, as if we weren't facing up to reality. Certainly there are forms of denial that can be destructive, such as the denial of alcoholics. Gay men who continue with high-risk sexual behavior are probably in denial about their vulnerability to AIDS. But in response to a life-threatening illness, this initial reaction enables you to continue functioning and take care of yourself as the news gradually filters through.

Denial can also be seen as selective attention. Men who are antibody positive often live for years without symptoms. There are men with ARC and AIDS who continue to work and whose condition has stabilized. Some men choose not to dwell on the possibility of worsening illness, and instead see themselves as "living with AIDS" as long and as well as they can. This determination to get on with life has been linked with improved immune functioning in the early stages of HIV infection.[2]

2. Bargaining

The notion behind bargaining is that you want to make some sort of deal (with fate, God, or the universe) to stave off the implications of a serious illness. You hope that by getting some exercise, eating better, and cutting out cigarettes and alcohol you'll build up your immune system. Aside from the obvious benefits of a healthier lifestyle, there is some evidence to suggest that exercise can stimulate immune functioning.[3]

3. Depression

A loved one with AIDS may become withdrawn and apathetic. He may wonder what's the point in trying anything when nothing he does seems to make any difference in his health or how he feels. The loss of familiar roles, such as being able to work or seeing oneself as young, strong, and physically attractive, can also lead to depression. Fatigue from the illness and from reactions to medication may contribute to social isolation.

4. Anger

A person with AIDS may get in touch with intense feelings of bitterness toward the unfairness and devastation of coming down with a life-threatening illness in the prime of his life. He may be angry at others who are well, enraged at whoever exposed him to this disease, and despise the government for doing so little. Internalized homophobia may resurface in the form of guilt and anger toward himself over past sexual behavior. Yet anger may also help bring him out of depression. Many persons with AIDS have been able to mobilize their anger to challenge the slow pace of research, inadequate drug trials, and lack of funding.

5. Acceptance

Acceptance can refer to a number of aspects: someone can accept that he actually has AIDS (or ARC or a positive antibody test) while still doing whatever he can to maintain his health. If he develops AIDS and over time his condition worsens, he may also acknowledge the possibility of dying. For some men, being able to talk about dying is a relief—they're no longer trying to protect loved ones from their own thoughts or fears. Others prefer to focus on what they've always enjoyed doing with friends, and don't want to dwell on the possibility of dying. There's no reason to push anyone toward acceptance as some final stage.

Many men have found a great deal of meaning in their lives

during the course of their illness, and a lot of this has to do with the quality of their relationships. They've inspired many of us to examine our own priorities and appreciate each day of our lives.

Reactions of the Partner

If your lover tests positive to HIV infection or receives an AIDS diagnosis, you may feel overwhelmed or numb and go through many of the stages we identified for one who is ill. You may also feel awkward and not know what to say. Life-threatening illness has been a taboo subject in our culture. We haven't developed very many norms about what you should say or how to react. But you don't have to know the "right" thing to say or come up with the most helpful response. Sometimes just being with someone can be a comfort. You may not need to say all that much right away—just listen to his feelings of numbness or devastation, and reach out to each other for support.

It he feels depressed, and nothing you do or say seems to affect how he feels, you may become impatient and wish he'd do something—get out more, see some friends, do whatever he's still physically capable of doing. But you can't always make someone feel better. If he feels despondent, just listen to his sorrow and pain. This can provide him with more support than if you immediately try to cheer him up, or get frustrated with him for feeling bad.

Similarly, you may catch some of the anger many of us feel about having to deal with this crisis. But that doesn't mean you have to feel so self-conscious that you withdraw altogether. Rather than becoming defensive or trying to talk him out of his feelings, it's helpful to acknowledge his anger. Having someone really understand how he feels can be a relief in itself.

Ill people are seldom touched and held. Physical contact can be very reassuring, especially to a person with AIDS, who may assume that others are afraid of him. Everyone has his own boundaries around touch; he may also be extremely tender because of his illness, or feel self-conscious about depending on others for personal care. You can be sensitive to his responses, and if you're not sure how he wants to be touched, you can always ask.

While taking care of him, you may feel overwhelmed by sorrow and fear in anticipating his loss. You wonder who will be there for you if your lover dies, especially if you become ill as well. You may find yourself pulling back and then feel guilty. You want to be strong, keep up hope, and always be available. Serious illness puts you both under quite a strain, and you can get on each other's nerves, despite your love for each other. You still need to take care of yourself, even while you're taking care of him. Get out and see your friends; go to a movie once in a while and pursue other interests. It may well be that you *can't* meet all his needs. It's important to get as much help as you can through friends and support services for attendant care, shopping, meals, and transportation.

Effects on Your Relationship

A diagnosis of AIDS can have a profound effect on your relationship. Your priorities will naturally shift, depending on whether he's able to keep on working or needs care at home. In the midst of taking him to medical exams and attending to practical details, it's easy to neglect your emotional reactions. Getting help from friends and other support services can help you keep in touch with each other emotionally.

Some men don't want to "give in" to sadness; they intend to get on with life. But it can be a relief to reach out to each other and acknowledge your feelings of sadness and concern. Being in touch with feelings won't take away from your ability to keep as well as you can. It actually takes a lot of effort to suppress feelings; pushing away sadness can leave you feeling depressed instead. Though our emotions can feel overwhelming, they aren't permanent. You may want to just hold each other at times, and let yourselves cry. You'll probably have more energy to fight the illness when you allow your feelings to wash over you now and then.

People with serious illness feel the loss of everyday interactions: they miss the humor, the conflict, and your usual cantankerousness. A partner who has AIDS doesn't necessarily want to be treated any differently. We needn't tiptoe around or talk about him as if he weren't in the same room (or talk *about* him in the other room). He'll want to be included in the rush of daily existence, just as he has always been.

Following his recovery from an opportunistic infection, the initial crisis is over, and most of your contingency plans are on hold. If he returns to work, it's difficult to believe he's still faced with a life-threatening illness. He may want to get on with the rest of his life and not be constantly identified with AIDS.

Just as you may shield him from some of your feelings, he may also feel guilty for being a burden to you, and worry about whether you resent him for being ill. You both may end up withholding feelings, and put on a cheerful front, because you don't want to let each other down. But with no one to confide in, you can end up feeling isolated from each other. You may prefer to voice some of your doubts and fears with a close friend, at a support group, or with a volunteer from one of the AIDS organizations. But you may find that, far from being a burden, you actually provide each other with more support when you say how you feel.

Withdrawal and Contact

In the following example we'll see how Vince and Carlos deal with their different desires for contact when Carlos isn't feeling well.

Carlos has swollen lymph nodes and other ARC symptoms. He started dating Vince, who lives around the corner, just a few months ago. They spend most nights together, but lately Carlos has had trouble sleeping, with night sweats and fevers. One night he tells Vince he'd rather sleep by himself. Vince says fine, and calls him the next morning.

VINCE: Hi, how are you doing?
CARLOS: I've been running a fever and didn't sleep much.
VINCE: I missed you.
CARLOS: I don't think I'd have been much fun to be around.
VINCE: You don't have to entertain me, you know.
CARLOS: I don't feel much like having company when I don't feel good.
VINCE: I know. You withdraw, right when I want to be helpful.
CARLOS: Well, you are being helpful.
VINCE: By staying away?

CARLOS: Yes. I'm rolling in sweat, and I'm in a lousy mood.

VINCE: You don't have to decide for me whether I want to be with you.

CARLOS: I'm just going to sleep all day.

VINCE: That's all right. If you like, I'll massage your back, or run some errands.

CARLOS: You're very sweet, but you really don't need to.

VINCE: But I want to. So is it all right to come over?

CARLOS: I guess I am trying to protect you.

VINCE: I like doing things for you.

CARLOS: It just feels simpler if you stay away; then I don't have to worry about you.

VINCE: You don't have to worry about me. It doesn't matter if you sleep all day; I just want to be around you.

Carlos lets Vince come over. Vince makes him some soup and then lies down with him for a while, rubbing his back when Carlos aches from fever. That evening, Vince says he'd like to spend the night.

CARLOS: I don't sleep well when you stay over.

VINCE: What if I brought in a cot?

CARLOS: I don't know, I don't want to bother—

VINCE: It's hard for you to believe I really want to stay with you, isn't it?

CARLOS: You've been here all day.

VINCE: I'm concerned about you spending the night by yourself.

CARLOS: If anything happens I'll call you.

VINCE: It's really no bother; I'll sleep on the couch.

CARLOS: But there's nothing to worry about.

VINCE: You're still doing it!

CARLOS: Doing what?

VINCE: You're still fending me off. I just want you to know that I care for you.

CARLOS: I know you care about me, but—

VINCE: It doesn't matter if you're drenched in sweat or in a lousy mood. I love you and want to be with you.

CARLOS: Oh.

Carlos has tears swimming in his eyes. Vince sits beside Carlos and caresses his forehead. "If you really want to be by yourself, I'll go. But you don't need to take care of me by sending me away."

It has been hard for Carlos to let Vince into his life, not wanting to burden him with his illness. Both partners can try to extend beyond their usual pattern—Carlos counters his tendency to withdraw by allowing Vince to care for him, and Vince accepts some limits to their time together. But, more important, they've opened a line of communication about their true feelings that will help them work through this conflict in the future.

Conflict over Treatment

Your lover has the right to make informed decisions about his illness. At the same time, he may feel frightened and overwhelmed by the onslaught of decisions that need to be made and the invasiveness of medical procedures. If his condition worsens, he may need to be hospitalized. If he's too sick to continue working, he may be laid off, lose his health insurance, and have to apply for disability. He may want to provide himself with as much self-care as possible, and resist help even when it's needed. You might want to break through what you see as denial because of your concern. But it's important for the person who is ill to retain as much control over treatment as possible. In the following example we'll look at how Doug and Stan deal with a conflict over treatment options.

Stan was diagnosed with pneumocystis a few months ago. He was treated on an outpatient basis, and returned to work shortly after. He receives pentamidine aerosol treatments to prevent a recurrence of pneumocystis, and for the most part he has done well since then. Just lately he has had a recurrence of candida, and a skin rash.

He's been following the research on AZT and other medications, but hasn't wanted to try them, preferring to investigate alternative healing practices. At first Doug supported Stan in whatever he wanted to do, but with Stan's recent symptoms, Doug has felt increasingly anxious.

DOUG: I think you'd better get on AZT.

STAN: I'm going to acupuncture this week, and I'm starting a new diet.

DOUG: I don't think that's enough. Why can't you do both?

STAN: I already told you, I'm taking care of it.

DOUG: You're not doing anything but going to a bunch of quacks!

STAN: Just bug off, Doug.

Stan resents Doug's judgments about alternative treatments, while Doug feels shut out. Doug realizes they're at an impasse. He backs off and acknowledges his part in escalating the argument.

DOUG: All right. I shouldn't put down alternative treatments. But I'm really worried.

STAN: Well, I am too. But we always end up arguing whenever we talk about treatment.

DOUG: That's true. Why don't we try using those steps for resolving conflicts so we can figure out how to deal with this.

Step 1: Clarify the Conflict

1a. Say what you'd like.

DOUG: I think you should go to the doctor and get evaluated for AZT.

STAN: I'd rather try alternative treatments.

1b. Distinguish desires from potential solutions. Rather than arguing, they try to identify their underlying desires. First Stan listens to Doug.

STAN: You're worried about this rash, aren't you?

DOUG: Yes! You hide it from me when you're not feeling well.

STAN: You don't want to be shut out.

DOUG: No, I want to be included in what's happening to you.

Then Doug listens to Stan.

STAN: Every time I say how I feel, you start in on me about AZT.

DOUG: You're tired of me bugging you about AZT.

STAN: So I figure why say anything; you're only going to worry and start giving me advice.

DOUG: You wish I'd just listen to how you feel, and not get on your case.

STAN: Yes! It's up to me what I want to do about it.

DOUG: You want control over your own treatment.

STAN: Of course. And I don't want to be a guinea pig for some AIDS researcher.

By listening and reflecting each other's concerns, they're able to identify their underlying desires.

Potential solution	Underlying desires
AZT versus alternative treatment	Keep Stan well Stan has control over treatment Doug wants to be included in Stan's care

1c. Identify behaviors and feelings; listen and reflect. They describe how they've each been affected by this pattern.

DOUG: You want my support, which I'm willing to give, but what you do also affects me. It's hard for me to just sit by and say "Fine, whatever" when I think you're being unrealistic about your care.

STAN: I'd like to include you, but you get so upset that it's easier not to say anything.

DOUG: I get more upset when you withdraw and stop talking to me.

STAN: I'd be more willing to tell you how I feel if you stopped pressuring me.

DOUG: You feel pressured when I suggest other treatments? I'm just trying to express my concern.

STAN: Don't you think I'm just as concerned as you are?

It may be that Doug has been carrying the concern for both of them. But Doug's suggestions felt intrusive, so Stan would withdraw, which left Doug feeling shut out. If Doug can listen without giving advice, Stan will feel less pressured. He'll be more open to discussing treatment options with Doug. When Doug feels included in Stan's care, he's able to identify his true fears.

DOUG: I'm sure diet and acupuncture can't hurt, but it makes me really nervous you're not doing anything else, especially since your candida came back.

STAN [looking at Doug and touching his arm]: You wish you could keep me well, don't you?

DOUG [choking up]: Yes. I'm so worried about what's going to happen.

STAN [putting his arm around him]: I am too, hon. [They hold each other for a long while.]

Behind much of their irritation with each other is sorrow and fear at the possibility of worsening illness. The decision over treatment options may still be difficult, but because they've acknowledged their mutual concern over Stan's health, they'll be more likely to provide each other the support they need to deal with whatever complications arise in the future.

Family Involvement

Informing your family is a major decision, and it's difficult to predict their reaction. Some are immediately supportive; some are openly hostile and rejecting, associating AIDS with a lifestyle they disapprove of; and many parents are so overwhelmed that they're really incapable of responding. You may actually end up having to support them.

If they find out you're gay at the same time they learn you've been diagnosed with AIDS, they may be so devastated that it will take some time for them to comprehend what this means for their son. They may be reluctant to discuss your illness with friends or relatives, and not know where to turn for accurate information.

It helps if you've already had time to sort through your own reactions before you tell them about your diagnosis. You'll be able to inform them about the nature of the syndrome and your course of treatment, allay fears about contagion, and let them know how they can be helpful.

Some gay men are alienated from their families and don't expect much help from them. They may even prefer not to inform them of their diagnosis. You really need to gauge for yourself how much support you can expect and whether you feel ready to deal with their reactions. You may have some idea how they'll react from their response to finding out you're gay. When confronted by the seriousness of their son's illness, some parents are able to move beyond their previous reservations about homosexuality and provide a great deal of support.

Dealing with family members who descend from all parts of the country can be stressful, both for the one who is ill and for his lover and friends. A parent who is insensitive to your relationship may attempt to take over decisions regarding care without consulting either you or your lover. Rather than seeing your partner or friends as a resource, some parents bar "nonfamily" visitors from the hospital.

Some hospitals will allow you to designate certain visitors, overruling your family's request. A "durable power of attorney for health care" is one method for designating your partner to assume medical decisions.[4] Though no one likes to consider the possibility of your condition worsening, this is something to anticipate before you become incapacitated. This will help ensure that your wishes are respected even if your parents attempt to take over.

Your family and partner may take out their frustrations on each other, and you can end up in the middle, trying to take care of everyone else. You, your partner, or a family therapist may be able to help you and your family recognize your common concerns. Despite initial reservations, and even open hostility, many family members and partners are able to include one another in their loved one's care.

Attitudes and Beliefs

A study of long-term AIDS survivors indicates that they have dealt with the syndrome in similar ways: they accept the diagnosis and are able to talk about it, while still fighting the illness; they assert their needs and get out of stressful or unproductive situations; they take personal responsibility for their health and see their physician as a collaborator; and they have helped others who have AIDS.[5] Studies of other illnesses, such as cancer, also indicate that a sense of hopefulness and active participation in your own care may increase your resistance to worsening illness.[6]

While it's tempting to conclude that anyone with AIDS should try to develop a "fighting spirit" in order to increase his chances for survival, it's useful to distinguish between correlations and causality. Though attitudes and beliefs can significantly affect one's quality of life, it may also be that long-term survivors are able to develop such a positive spirit because they have lived and dealt with AIDS over an extended period of time.

Some men respond to an AIDS diagnosis with a determination to fight the disease, while others are emotionally devastated. It takes a great deal of support to mobilize oneself to the extent outlined above. A person with AIDS needs our attention and love, whether he feels optimistic or despondent. To imply that his illness is the result of a negative attitude or a failure of will can be pretty demoralizing. He's more likely to feel cared for when we're able to listen to him, without discounting either his doubts or his hopefulness.

Even the health of someone who has a positive outlook and has participated in his own care may deteriorate. Acknowledging this possibility to himself or to others won't undermine his determination to stay as well as he can; rather, it can help him avoid blaming himself if his condition worsens.

Life-threatening illness touches on our most profound beliefs about the nature of existence. Whenever a disease of mysterious origin strikes a community, all sorts of ideas spring up about what it means and how to protect ourselves.[7] Having a particular attitude or belief can help us make sense of what's happening to us and give us hope. You can support your partner's enthusiasm in fighting his illness and still be able to listen to his concerns if he feels discouraged.

Being with a Lover While He Is Dying

If your partner is hospitalized with recurring infections, ends up on a respirator, and is being fed through a tube or intravenously, he may want to make some decisions about the measures he wants taken if his heart fails or other vital signs collapse (see "Quality of Life," below). If he thinks he's approaching the end, he may want to gather people around him, or he may prefer to be alone or with you. It may be difficult for you, your friends, and family to grasp that he may soon be leaving you.

Dementia is a common complication with AIDS; it can leave a person feeling disoriented and confused by memory lapses. His world may constrict, so that previous interests no longer matter; or he may imagine that he's still occupied with whatever was important to him in the past. Even people with dementia have more lucid moments, so his condition should not totally exclude him from decisions about his care. He may have some surprising insights, such as knowing who can best attend to specific needs and how certain people will relate to him. He may sense that others are not ready to face his loss, and he may need some reassurance that you're taking care of yourself, so he can let go when he needs to.

Eventually every relationship comes to an end: the one who is dying loses everyone and everything he has ever known—and you're left behind to deal with his loss without him. He may wish to tell you something, or simply have you close to him. Even in a coma, when he's not able to respond, he may still be able to hear and be aware of what's going on around him. It's helpful for loved ones to be able to express their love and memories and say good-bye—whether in words, meditation, touch, or prayer—not only for his sake, but as a part of your own process of letting go and mourning his loss. Simply being there for each other at this final parting can provide you with a heartfelt sense of connection for the rest of your life.

Grieving

Grief is not limited to the actual loss of someone close to us; it often begins in anticipation of the loss. Some people are immediately in touch with a torrent of grief when they first hear of someone diagnosed with AIDS. Or they may experience an initial numbness, followed by bargaining, depression, and anger.

For someone who has assumed a lot of responsibility for the care of a loved one through a protracted illness, the actual death may leave him feeling strangely relieved, as well as sad and empty. His entire life for the last several months may have revolved around taking care of his partner. He may feel guilty for moments when he looked forward to the time when this ordeal would finally be over.

Even at the end of this intense level of involvement, there may be a lot of loose ends to take care of. He seems to be on "automatic" as he handles the details of funeral arrangements, deals with relatives, and handles the estate. But gradually there's not as much to do anymore; going back to work or taking care of the house can seem mundane, even meaningless. He thought he had already used up his capacity for grief in anticipating his lover's death. But weeks, even months later, he finds himself entering another cycle of mourning—intrusive thoughts and dreams, feelings of sorrow, and waves of aching sadness may arise at unpredictable moments.

Everyone grieves at his own pace; there really isn't a specific timetable for when you will feel altogether healed. Just when you think you've adjusted, a song, a familiar smell, or an anniversary may plunge you into the depths of your sorrow. Though each plunge may feel as deep, over time you may be able to emerge a little more rapidly, and not feel quite so overwhelmed. It may be many months, or even years, before a day goes by without some thought or memory of your loved one.

Many gay men have lost a lover, a number of close friends, and perhaps dozens of acquaintances. Each new death adds to the well of unexpressed grief, to a point where our community as a whole may feel numbed to it. We may become impatient with a friend's sorrow, and wish he'd just "get over it." This is because we're reminded of our own losses and pain. Our feelings and memories are all part of the grieving process. It helps to express our grief, rather than pushing it away.

Every culture has mourning rituals, which help its members acknowledge the profound meaning of their loss. For gay men, a lack of recognition for the importance of our relationships can be demoralizing. The workplace may not allow time off for a funeral, and families may deny that our loss is equivalent to the death of a spouse.

Many gay men have created their own memorials, such as the AIDS Quilt, which affirm and celebrate our relationships.[8] You can also share memories with friends—bring out photographs, talk about when you first met, and remember how you used to tease each other. You might want to say or write down whatever you never got around to telling him while he was still alive.

When should you be concerned that you might need some assistance, apart from friends or peer counseling resources, to deal with your loss? You can expect to be incapacitated for a while, but if, over an extended period of time, you're just not able to take care of yourself, it may be a good idea to seek professional counseling. The following signs should alert you to the need for additional support: neglecting personal hygiene or staying in bed much of the time; overworking, drinking, or engaging in unsafe sexual behavior; and prolonged feelings of worthlessness or suicidal thoughts.

The grieving process involves a gradual acceptance of the death, with an eventual readiness for new relationships.[9] Even these relationships can be tinged by the memory of your former lover. Your new partner may need some reassurance about his importance in your life now, with him.

Suicidal Thoughts

Suicidal ideas, if not the intent to act on them, are common among people who are faced with a life-threatening illness (as well as people who are grieving over a significant loss). These thoughts and impulses fall into three broad areas, which can certainly overlap: panic following an initial diagnosis; despair in the depths of depression; and a consideration of "quality of life" when someone's health continues to deteriorate.

Panic
A diagnosis of AIDS (ARC or a positive antibody test) can precipitate a crisis. One's usual ability to absorb information and figure out what to do next is overwhelmed; he sees suicide as the "only" way out of a desperate situation, and may act impulsively. This is a panic-stricken reaction to devastating news.

Despair
Feelings of despair and hopelessness can arise at other times in the course of a serious illness. He may become depressed in

response to a spread of lesions, rehospitalization for a new infection, the death of a friend, or severe side effects from medication. Depression is a common response to life-threatening illness, but severe, ongoing depression arising out of hopelessness and despair should be evaluated for treatment.

A depressed person who is considering suicide may be vague about his intent—he might say "What's the use in trying anymore," or communicate his plan indirectly by giving away significant possessions. Don't be afraid to ask someone if he's thinking of killing himself—it doesn't "put ideas into his head." If he's not considering it, he'll just say "No." If he is, our asking will reassure him that we won't recoil in fear or disgust, and he may be more willing to talk about it.

There's a difference between feeling so bad he wants to kill himself and actually trying to do so. Suicidal thoughts may simply be an expression of how bad he feels. Most people considering suicide are ambivalent. Being able to express himself may give him enough perspective so he won't feel the need to act on his impulse.

When listening to someone who is suicidal, it's useful in your own mind to separate feelings, thoughts, and behavior: the feeling is sadness or despair, the thought is that his condition is hopeless, and the potential behavior is trying to harm himself. Friends may be so disturbed by suicidal ideas that they try to talk him out of feeling bad: they point out all the things he has to live for and try to cheer him up. But discounting his feelings tends to make him think you don't really understand him. He will tend to polarize with you, or withdraw. You don't need to talk him out of feeling sad. It can be a tremendous relief just to have someone listen and really understand how despairing he feels. Once he feels understood, he may not see his situation as completely hopeless.

If he has a plan and the means to carry it out, and he refuses to put it off, he has a very high risk of hurting himself. Encourage him to get some help by calling a crisis clinic or suicide prevention. You can offer to call, or take him yourself. If he won't talk to a hotline worker over the phone, refuses to go with you to a clinic, and still intends to kill himself, you can also call the police, who will take him to a crisis center to be evaluated. If he's unable to agree not to *act* on his despair for a specified length of time (for example, until his next appointment), a mental health professional will need to set limits on his impulse to commit suicide. Hospitalization for suicidal ideation doesn't mean he's "crazy"; it's simply a time-out to make sure he's kept safe until he can remobilize his coping skills.

The main goals in dealing with a suicidal crisis are to acknowledge the feelings (which is often enough to alleviate the suicidal impulse) and, if he's still intent on killing himself, to take whatever steps are needed to ensure his safety while he's feeling overwhelmed.

Quality of Life

A desire to end one's suffering may arise from a rapidly deteriorating condition and the assumption that he's not likely to recover. Increased pain, blindness, and physical disability can also precipitate suicidal thoughts. He might have assumed he'd want to "check out" by now, yet sometimes his feelings change in response to the quality of attention he receives from loved ones. Significant advances in pain control may also keep his level of discomfort within a more tolerable range.

There are some who would like to control how and when they die. They come up against the fact that our laws are still largely geared to the assumption that anyone who wants to end his life is operating out of a crisis mode or depression. No one may assist in another's suicide; by law, medical and psychological staff must take steps to prevent it.

There is some leeway, however, in the final stages of terminal illness. Some states allow hospitalized patients to designate "no code," which means they won't be resuscitated if vital functions fail and no "extraordinary measures" will be used to keep them alive. You can also refuse invasive procedures or further treatment. While it's illegal to administer lethal doses of medication for the purpose of euthanasia, your physician (in consultation with you and your partner) may increase your pain medication to keep you as comfortable as possible. At high doses, a secondary effect of increased pain medication can be a cessation of vital functions.

The notion of whether it's possible to commit a rational suicide is an unresolved area in psychiatric and medical ethics. It reflects the ambivalence in our society over the right to a conscious decision about death. This may gradually change as we evaluate our expanding ability to prolong life, and the implications this has for the quality of our final days.

Living with AIDS

While not ignoring the possibility of worsening illness, many men with HIV infection take care of themselves, contribute to others, and challenge the delays in drug trials and funding. They focus on wellness and do the best they can to live a normal existence.

Researchers are increasingly optimistic over extending the life of persons with AIDS.[10] Dr. Anthony Fauci of the National Institutes of Health predicts that some persons with AIDS "may live a lifetime with the disease."[11] At the Fourth International Conference on AIDS, Dr. Gerald Friedland said effective therapies are available now for the majority of HIV disease symptoms, and Dr. Robert Redfield said, "Eradication of HIV is within the grasp of man."[12]

Most gay men, especially in large urban areas, have gotten past an initial denial that we're vulnerable to AIDS. We've accepted the seriousness of what we're faced with, and we're doing what we can to prevent its spread. A balance of hopefulness and realism is difficult to maintain; most of us slide from one extreme to the other at times. We can listen to one another's fears and support one another in our hopes. What we've managed to deal with so far is only a glimpse of the challenge our entire society will face in the years to come. We can pull together to expand our model of caring to include everyone affected by this syndrome, helping them live with AIDS for as long and as well as they can.

Questions and Comments

Q: I was diagnosed two years ago, and I don't have much energy to do things outside of the house. My lover turns down friends' invitations, saying he has to take care of me. How can I convince him it's all right for him to go out?

A: He may feel guilty for going out when you can't join him. Tell him you don't expect him to stay home all the time, and listen to his concern about your care if he leaves the house. Make arrangements for respite care, attendants, and friends to help out. You both need a break from each other now and then; it's impossible to do everything on your own without getting on each other's nerves. You might also want to consider what kind of support you would need in order to go someplace together.

Q: My best friend's lover died very suddenly only a month after diagnosis. Since then his life has been a total wreck—he stopped going to work, he's lost a lot of weight, and hasn't been taking care of himself. Lately he's been getting out more, but he's having unsafe sex, even though he's been seronegative. How can I talk some sense into him?

A: He may be unable to make sense of why his lover was infected and he wasn't. He could be experiencing "survivor guilt," punishing himself for his lover's death. Encourage him to go to a grief support group, individual psychotherapy, or Sex and Love Addicts Anonymous. He needs some help right away, especially to stop his high-risk sexual behavior.

Q: My lover was diagnosed a few months ago and is doing fairly well. His parents are coming to visit, but he doesn't want to tell them he has AIDS. They've always been supportive of our relationship, and it feels awkward to me to pretend nothing is wrong. He doesn't want me to tell my family, either, though I'd like their support for myself. I said it would be worse for them to find out when he's hospitalized, and he got pissed off.

A: Informing one's family of an AIDS diagnosis is a very personal decision. But since you know his parents, and you also want support from your own family, his decision obviously affects you as well. If he intends to inform them about his diagnosis eventually, it's probably better to wait until he has had time to absorb the news, but not so long that they end up finding out in the midst of a medical crisis.

Listen to each other's feelings and identify your underlying desires. Maybe he doesn't want to burden his family, or he's not ready to deal with their reactions. When you empathize with him, you'll help him sort through his feelings about his illness and what it would mean for him to tell his family. Seeing you as an ally, rather than an adversary, will help him consider your need for support as well.

P A R T

SEEKING
HELP

He finds a comrade—
Now he pounds the drum, now he stops.
Now he sobs; now he sings.
—CHUNG FU/INNER TRUTH, FROM THE *I CHING*

11

Couples Therapy

Though this book is intended to help you resolve conflicts on your own, there may be times when you both feel so emotionally charged that you have a hard time listening to each other, and every effort to deal with your conflict seems to make it worse. In this chapter we'll identify problems that indicate you could use professional assistance and outline what you can expect in couples counseling.[1]

When to Get Help

There will naturally be rough spots in any relationship; not every conflict means you need therapy. You can get a lot of help by talking with friends and other couples about how they've worked through various issues. But sometimes what you try on your own isn't enough, and you find yourselves caught in a cycle of escalating anger, withdrawal, and suspicion. Any of the following problems is a strong indication that you could use some professional help to make it through hard times:

1. You're consistently unable to listen to each other without interrupting.
2. The same conflict repeats itself, and you're unable to reach any lasting resolution.

3. Your perceptions about your problems are mutually disconfirming—you end up thinking "If he's right, I must be crazy."
4. You don't feel safe bringing up certain topics.
5. You're abusing alcohol or drugs, or engaging in other compulsive behaviors (sex, eating, debt, gambling, work).
6. Arguments escalate into emotional or physical abuse.
7. Either partner is depressed for a prolonged time or feels suicidal.

If any of these signs persist, it's wise to seek professional assistance.

As men, we're raised to think we should be able to handle problems on our own. We also tend to rationalize our feelings, and this inhibits us from seeking assistance when we're in emotional pain. We figure there's really no "reason" to be upset, so we ignore our feelings or deny we're hurting. But our pain tends to express itself through withdrawal, depression, or angry outbursts.

Just as you don't wait for your car to break down before you change the oil or have a tune-up, you don't have to wait until you're totally fed up with each other to get some help. Couples counseling is not an admission of failure, any more than getting a valve job. Someone who has worked a great deal with emotional fine-tuning in relationships can provide some pointers about where you're missing each other. You can also use couples counseling to maintain or even enhance your ability to communicate in your realtionship.

What to Expect in Couples Counseling

Some hesitancy to enter couples therapy comes from simply not knowing what to expect. No one wants to feel blamed for everything that has gone wrong in a relationship. The therapist's role is not to judge who's right or wrong, but to help you clarify what you want from each other and identify patterns that get in your way.

Couples counseling provides the safety of a controlled interaction in which you can both feel understood. The therapist helps you stay in contact with each other and work through conflicts even when you're angry, without the fear that you'll escalate out of control. You'll learn to identify specific behaviors you're upset about; clarify the feelings behind your interpretations; discover the desires that underlie potential solutions; and perceive the positive intent behind your hurt, anger, and disappointment. The therapist helps you consolidate these skills so you can resolve future conflicts on your own.

Phases in Couples Counseling

I have identified the following phases in my therapy with male couples. Though therapists work in a variety of ways, these phases can give you a general idea of what you're likely to encounter in couples counseling.

Entry Phase

The initial phase consists of gathering information, setting goals, and establishing ground rules for therapy. I want to know what both men's backgrounds were like, so we can identify the expectations they bring to the relationship from their families. I ask them when they realized they were gay and how they feel about it now. What was it about each partner that attracted them? How did they initiate contact? When did they first identify themselves as a couple? This helps set a cooperative tone for therapy, by reminding them of how they got involved with each other in the first place.

To elicit some goals for treatment, I ask them how they'd like things to have changed once we've finished our work together. I help them formulate these goals in terms of positive behaviors, such as "improved communication," rather than "I want him to stop manipulating me." Depending on their goals, I'll suggest we make a commitment to meet for a specified period of time (usually twelve to sixteen sessions).

During the course of treatment feelings will likely surface that lead them to question whether this is really going to work. Dealing with current problems and clearing out old resentments can feel pretty threatening. They may not feel confident that they'll be able to work through these disagreements, and hesitate to say what's really bothering them for fear they'll just make things worse. By having a commitment to continue for a specific number of sessions, they know they'll have the chance to work through whatever feelings arise in therapy. At the end of this period, we evaluate their progress and renegotiate more time if it is needed.

Before getting into the heart of their conflict, I establish the following ground rules:

1. Both partners will come to every session. Feeling demoralized or pessimistic is not a reason to stay away. They agree to come and talk about feeling demoralized, instead of acting out this feeling by not coming to therapy.
2. There will be no violence or threats of violence during or between sessions (see chapter 14 for how to get help for battering relationships).
3. Any communication to the therapist by either of them, whether by phone or letter or in person, will be acknowledged to his partner in the next session. Though one partner may feel more comfortable confiding in the therapist, it's useless information unless we can bring it back to the couple's session and deal with it there.
4. If either partner feels very upset, I will encourage him to talk about what's upsetting him, rather than leaving the session early.

This phase of gathering information, setting goals, and establishing ground rules usually takes one or two sessions.

Ventilating Resentments

When entering treatment, both partners are often angry and hurt. At last they have a safe place to ventilate their feelings. If they're too upset to listen to each other, I do most of the listening myself. I reflect what I've heard, to make sure I've understood both partners. Once they feel calmer, I teach the listening and sending skills described in Part 1, and help them practice with neutral topics. Then we move back into current issues. I encourage each man to speak for himself, rather than interpreting or analyzing his partner. I help them identify the feelings behind their interpretations and express their complaints in terms of behaviors and feelings.

Each partner will paraphrase what he's heard, until they can both acknowledge they've been understood. I emphasize that listening does not mean compliance and understanding does not equal agreement. We clarify their conflict by identifying the underlying desires that they want a potential solution to address, and we continue to follow the steps for resolving conflicts outlined in chapter 4.

Toward the end of this phase, we're usually able to identify the positive intent that underlies their distress—the reason for their disappointment, anger, and hurt is that they really do care for each other, and this realization motivates them to work through their conflicts.

Honeymoon
After acknowledging their desire to stay together, they may be more willing to cooperate. They negotiate agreements during our sessions, and "try to do better" during the week. They anticipate each other's needs and begin to feel optimistic about their progress. They neglect their practice of listening and sending skills, and question whether it's necessary to continue in couples therapy. I hold out for keeping our original commitment, and encourage their skill-building sessions during the week, even if everything seems rosy.

Falling Out
Then something happens to precipitate a crisis: the recurrence of a previous pattern, an argument, or a violation of one of their agreements. One feels betrayed, the other unjustly accused, all the more so because of the recent impression that everything was working fine. What happened? Was this all an illusion?

The realization that they still loved each other seemed enough to carry them through any difficulty they could imagine. While their love can serve as a fine motivation for making things work, they may have been trying to accommodate each other, rather than really coming to terms with some of their differences. Resentments build until they have a falling out.

They may feel pessimistic about resolving their differences, and question why they're even bothering with counseling. Again, it's important that they've made a commitment to meet for a certain length of time, so that their discouragement doesn't bring a premature end to treatment.

Working Through

They want to feel better about each other; these skills seem simple enough, so what happened? It's easy to become suspicious of each other's sincerity about really wanting the relationship to work. I may become quite active again in helping them clarify their feelings: their disappointment, fears, and hopes.

Good intentions need to be translated into a more realistic acknowledgement of their differences, and we begin the work of sorting through various conflicts. During this phase we clarify the function of their conflicts and discover how each partner contributes to the patterns that have developed between them. We develop fresh ways for them to approach these problems by talking about the pattern, rather than rehashing the conflict.

Since eventually they'll be on their own, I encourage them to practice their communication skills during the week. I want to make sure they have the tools to handle future conflicts, once couples therapy has ended.

Termination

In the last few sessions we assess what they've accomplished and try to anticipate whatever difficulties might arise as their relationship develops. Just as seeking assistance in the first place is not an admission of failure, returning for couples work is left open as an option for additional support if they'd like some assistance at some point in the future.

When you're caught in the middle of an unsatisfying interaction, it's natural to doubt whether you're really compatible. Couples therapy can provide you with tools to identify these patterns and work through your underlying conflicts. By learning how to express your feelings and empathize with your partner, you'll rediscover some of the qualities that attracted you to each other in the first place.

Questions and Comments

Q: I'd like to go into couples counseling, but my lover refuses to go. He says, "You're the one with the problem."

A: He may think he has to admit there's something wrong with him before he can seek help. It's useful to think of the "problem," whatever it is, as existing *between* you, in the relationship. It's not necessary to assign blame or think there's something wrong with you in order to recognize that something is not working between you.

Therapists often end up seeing a couple after they've worked with one partner, who is trying to figure out how he feels and what he wants to do about his relationship. Over time it becomes clear that it would be more useful to work with both of them. With his client's permission, the therapist will invite his partner to join them. Sometimes the first man says, "Oh, he'll never come," and occasionally that's true. But often his lover has seen some changes in his partner and is willing to give it a try.

It may be just as well for them to see another therapist for couples work, especially if the first man has issues he wants to continue in individual treatment.

Q: I think we could use some counseling, but I'm not sure I even want to stay in this relationship. I don't want to feel pressured to continue if it's not working.

A: Some men come to couples counseling so discouraged they're not sure they want to remain a couple. The goal in therapy is not necessarily to stay together, but to communicate your desires effectively. This will allow you to come to your own conclusion about whether you want to continue your relationship.

Even if you decide to split up, it helps to have worked this through, rather than breaking off simply because you were annoyed with each other and couldn't think of any other way to express your dissatisfaction. By staying until the end, you'll have a chance to understand what you both contributed to the problems that developed between you, and you'll be able to communicate more clearly about what you want in your next relationship.

Paradoxically, some couples feel differently toward each other after they seriously consider breaking up. They're able to empathize with how hard it has been, and this motivates them to try again.

Q: My lover wanted to go into couples counseling and I agreed, assuming we were trying to salvage our relationship. But he sabotaged whatever agreements we came up with. When the therapist pointed this out, he finally copped to the fact that he'd already made up his mind to leave the relationship.

A: Sometimes one man wants out but can't bring himself to say so; his guilt may inhibit his own awareness, or he feels ambivalent. The course of therapy can help him clarify his feelings. If he violates agreements, he essentially forces his partner to reject him instead. This can be pointed out, so that he can say what's bothering him instead of acting out his feelings.

Couples often wait until they're on the verge of splitting up before they seek help. It can be a relief to have the safety of a controlled interaction in which they can explore how they really feel. But therapy is no miracle cure: it takes some persistent effort to understand each other, resolve conflicts, and follow through on agreements.

12

Alcohol and Drugs

*H*uman beings have a natural capacity for altered states of consciousness, which occur spontaneously throughout the day as we make love, exercise, sleep, or daydream. You often see kids spinning each other silly, or holding their breath until they're dizzy.[1] Every culture throughout history has developed certain rituals for expanding awareness, whether through meditation, fasting, physical ordeals, prayer, or chemical substances.[2] Understanding that altered states occur naturally can help us normalize our desire for profound experience and free us from the assumption that we need to take a drug in order to expand our consciousness.

The problem we face today is that the proliferation of refined substances has overwhelmed society's capacity to handle their effects. Highly refined substances are more likely to be abused than the herbs from which they were originally derived. And when a chemical becomes separated from its ritualized function, either through disruption of the society or by being introduced to a new culture, it has a higher potential for abuse.[3] We also live in a fractured culture in which many people take drugs to escape from emotional pain. These factors greatly increase the likelihood of developing a problematic relationship with chemical substances.

Use versus Abuse

Most people use some mind-altering substance occasionally, whether it's wine with dinner or coffee with dessert. Addiction to alcohol or other drugs is a progressive condition; no one starts out in the gutter, and most people who use substances never end up there. Though many people deny that their use of substances is a problem even when it interferes with work and interpersonal relations, some people maintain a controlled use of potentially addictive chemicals without becoming psychologically or physically dependent.[4]

Alcohol is by far the most seriously abused substance (followed closely by prescribed medications), yet the focus of much of the public's concern has been on illegal drugs. This reflects our cultural denial of the hazards of alcohol and prescription drug abuse. So how do we distinguish use from abuse, apart from social custom or arbitrary moral standards? The following phases can help you gauge your own level of involvement with alcohol and other substances.[5]

Discovering That Chemicals Can Affect Moods
In the first phase you learn that certain chemicals can help you relax, wake up, go to sleep, escape, get high, or calm down. They provide a disinhibiting feeling of well-being and pleasure. Your usual cares and worries recede in importance. You feel more confident, and your insights seem profound.

Going After the High
In the second phase you experiment with different quantities, and you experience some physical consequences (such as a hangover) when you overindulge. You set some rules for yourself about how much you will use and under what circumstances: you discover how much to drink without getting drunk; you use substances only with friends, on social occasions; and you don't drive under the influence. This is what people often refer to as "social drinking" or use.

People who are able to *maintain* these rules usually don't go on to develop a substance abuse problem. But if you're consistently using alcohol or other chemicals to have sex, to feel comfortable in social situations, or generally to feel better about yourself, then it's inhibiting the development of other coping skills. Instead of learning how to deal with daily pressures, it seems easier to drink, smoke, or take a pill.

You may not think you're progressing toward dependency, but you're establishing a pattern that could worsen in the face of a major disappointment. The loss of your job, the end of a relationship, or the death of your lover can trigger episodic substance abuse if you've grown accustomed to using chemicals as a way of dealing with uncomfortable feelings.

Dependency

As tolerance increases, you can easily slide into psychological dependence on the drug. You have a drink and feel relaxed, less inhibited, and more sociable. You find it easier to be amused. Interestingly enough, this is often how people feel when they're around someone they trust. Drinking or getting stoned may be a way of capturing a similar glow of camaraderie, even if you don't really trust the people you're with. It may seem like far less work than learning how to feel more comfortable around people, or finding closer friends. You can drink, and lose yourself in the illusion.

Previous rules are broken: you use more than you intended; you begin using alone; you drive while drunk. You can no longer predict how much you're going to use or how you might behave. You end up violating your own values while intoxicated, and these incidents undermine your self-esteem. This makes you increasingly more vulnerable to using drugs or alcohol to push negative feelings away. Your world may seem so unpleasant that you'd like to escape. The world is still there when you come back, and in the meantime you've avoided learning what it takes to cope with unpleasant feelings.

Using Just to Feel Normal

You begin to organize your life around your substance of choice. You drop friends who don't share your preoccupation with getting high. Work and interpersonal relationships begin to suffer. You blame others for your own failings and inadequacies. As physical dependency develops, you're able to drink more without getting drunk. You no longer experience euphoric mood swings. As you continue toward habituation and physical addiction, you gradually discover that, far from getting high, you need a certain amount of drugs just to feel normal. You experience blackouts more frequently, go on binges, and deteriorate physically. You have no sense of purpose, and nothing to look forward to but the next fix.

Denial

In the face of obvious deterioration and emotional pain, you're able to deny you have a problem through blackouts, repression, and euphoric recall.[6]

Blackouts
Blackouts are chemically induced gaps in memory. They are unpredictable in terms of how much substance it takes to cause one, when it will take place, or how long it will last. Memory loss shields you from recognizing your abusive relationship with the chemical, because you don't recall self-destructive or embarrassing behavior.

Repression
Repression is a defense against a loss in self-esteem. It makes you less aware of uncomfortable feelings, and it also inhibits your memory of behavior you would ordinarily find shameful.

Euphoric Recall
Euphoric recall distorts your perception of what your behavior was really like—you may remember the glow of your subjective experience and not the actual behavior you exhibited. You bask in a memory of camaraderie, wit, and emotional closeness that is essentially delusional. Far from thinking you were the life of the party, others who weren't intoxicated may remember your behavior as oafish, alienating, and rude.

Causes of Substance Abuse

Alcoholism and other addictive behaviors are thought to arise from three main sources (which are not mutually exclusive):

genetic predisposition, social conditioning, and psychological factors.

Genetic Predisposition

Some people seem to metabolize alcohol differently, and this may predispose them to abuse by setting off a physiological craving in response to small amounts of alcohol.

Social Conditioning

Many people who develop a problem with alcohol have parents who were alcoholics. This family link may have more to do with the dynamics that occur in alcoholic families than it does with inheritance.[7] The child learns that alcohol is how adults cope with emotional stress.

Social conditioning may also explain why gay men, as an oppressed group, have a higher incidence of alcohol abuse.[8] Homophobia in our society has limited our ability to meet each other safely. The bar culture arose from our desire to have a place where we could expect to find other gay men, without the harassment or threats that might ensue if we approached a man who turned out to be heterosexual.

As the gay subculture developed around the bar scene, alcohol came to be associated with gay liberation and having a good time. It eased our inhibitions about having sex with men, and bars may have been the first place where many of us felt truly accepted for who we were.

Psychological Factors

Drugs and alcohol are commonly used to push feelings away, but those feelings are still there. As mentioned earlier, we tend to act out the feelings we're not consciously aware of. Instead of feeling hurt, for example, someone might get drunk and try to humiliate his partner. Anger and sadness may be turned inward through self-destructive behavior.

Feelings continue to press for recognition. When the effects of the drug wear off, you can feel bored, anxious, irritable, or depressed. These are secondary feelings, masking sadness, fear, and hurt. But you never get to these primary feelings when you drink or take drugs to ward them off.

Once you've learned that alcohol can momentarily allow you to feel better about yourself, you may stop learning other ways to handle uncomfortable feelings. Alcohol lowers inhibitions and can mask the shame stemming from internalized homophobia. If you haven't learned how to feel good about yourself sober, it may be difficult to have sex or feel close to another man unless you get high.

When you shut off unpleasant feelings, eventually good feelings shut down as well. The process of recovery allows you to heal by working through the feelings that you pushed away by using drugs. Allowing your emotions to surface eventually changes them. You're no longer controlled by unconscious feelings, and you no longer need drugs or alcohol to push unpleasant feelings away.

Getting Help

The first step toward getting help is realizing that substance abuse is a problem. For the reasons outlined above, this is not always easy, because your view of the problem may be distorted by an unreliable memory. But if you're honest with yourself, and willing to accept loved ones' feedback about your behavior, you may be able to break through this denial and recognize when you're having a problem.

Using alcohol as an example, ask yourself the following questions as a gauge for whether your substance use may be getting in the way of work, interpersonal relationships, or other interests:[9]

1. Have you ever wondered whether you have a drinking problem?
2. Do you ever end up drinking more than you intended?
3. Have you had periods of time while you were drinking that you couldn't remember later?
4. Have you ever had hassles with friends, gotten in trouble at work, or been arrested as a result of drinking?
5. Do you find yourself looking forward to the time of day when you usually have a drink?
6. Do you feel irritated when other people comment on how much you drink?

If you think you might be abusing alcohol or other substances, Alcoholics Anonymous and Narcotics Anonymous can help you with the process of recovery. Some people feel resistant to going to AA, because it breaks through their denial that alcohol is a problem. They may be more embarrassed by the thought of being seen at an AA meeting than they were by various behaviors while drunk that they regretted later.

Though some people manage to stop for a while on their own, they're often "white-knuckling" it, hanging on until the next crisis puts them over the edge. Recovery doesn't have so much to do with willpower as with learning other strategies for coping with the feelings that were pushed away while you leaned on alcohol. AA and other twelve-step programs provide a community of support, in which you can learn how to handle the feelings that emerge once you're no longer pushing them away with drugs or alcohol. There are groups all across the country, with gay meetings in many cities. Even in areas where there are no gay meetings, most gay men find AA nonjudgmental toward our lifestyle.

If you have become physically addicted, safe withdrawal from high doses of some drugs (alcohol and Valium, for example) may require a detoxification program supervised by a physician. Call your local drug rehabilitation center for advice before detoxing on your own.

Therapists commonly insist that clients not be using any substance as a condition of therapy. You agree not to get high before coming to therapy, since "no one's home" to do therapy with if you're loaded. And if drug or alcohol use, has been a problem in the past, the therapist may also insist that you not be using at all, even *between* therapy sessions. This is because there's little motivation to learn to deal with the feelings that emerge in therapy if you can always escape by getting high.

Recovery

If you have a substance abuse problem, your emotional development essentially stopped when you began using. You're accustomed to self-medicating your feelings, so you never learned how to handle disappointments and conflicts. When you're no longer using, you're thrown back on yourself, with few emotional re-sources to cope with the sudden onrush of feelings you managed to push away for many years.

For much of the first year or two in recovery, you'll feel buffeted by your emotions. Rage and sorrow can alternate with boredom and restlessness. Before you get in touch with your natural rhythms or interests, you don't know what to look forward to, and your life can seem meaningless. In recovery groups you will hear others talk about how they got through this stage, one day at a time. Gradually you become more accustomed to dealing with your feelings and less vulnerable to dramatic mood swings. With the support of others, you begin to trust the gradual pace of natural growth that takes place while you heal.

Substance Abuse in Relationships

Obviously the turmoil of the initial stages of recovery can have profound effects on your relationship, especially if your partner is still using, or if he grew up in an alcoholic family himself.

If you protect your partner from the consequences of his abuse by covering up for him or pretending there really isn't a problem, you become part of his denial system. While you can't *make* someone else stop drinking or using, you can set limits to his behavior, so you're not reinforcing his abuse. This is difficult to do on your own—you can get support from Al-anon, Adult Children of Alcoholics, and codependency groups.

Al-anon
Al-anon is for anyone who's in a close relationship with an alcoholic, even if you didn't grow up in an alcoholic family yourself. This program teaches you how to avoid getting caught up in your partner's denial. You realize that you can't control anyone else's life; you can only control your own.

Adult Children of Alcoholics
Children of alcoholic parents often become "parentified children" in their own families, taking on responsibilities that no child should have to assume: they try to support their parents emotion-ally, take over household tasks, and look after other siblings

while their parents are drunk or otherwise emotionally unavailable. While one child is desperately trying to hold everything
together, the other children may start drinking or using themselves, get in trouble with the law, or tune out altogether.

Claudia Black identifies three messages kids receive from
alcoholic (or other dysfunctional) families: don't trust, don't talk,
and don't feel.[10]

1. *Don't trust.* Don't trust others, especially outside the family—and most important of all, don't trust yourself or your own
perceptions. What you think is happening around you isn't really
happening at all. If you get beat up or molested, it's your own
fault.

2. *Don't talk.* Don't acknowledge that alcohol is a problem
within the family, and don't let anyone outside the family know
the family secret. An example frequently cited in AA meetings is
"Let's pretend the rampaging rhinoceros in the living room isn't
really there." This pattern of secrecy also occurs with incest,
ridicule, and violence.

3. *Don't feel.* Through various put-downs after expressing
yourself, you learn to suppress your feelings—they don't count,
no one will listen to you anyway, and expressing your feelings
will only get you into trouble. You believe that it's wrong to have
negative feelings and that "real men" don't cry.

Children from alcoholic families grow up in a dysfunctional
situation, and they develop certain skills in order to survive.
These skills needn't be discarded in the course of recovery, but
you can develop other abilities in order to achieve a balance in
intimate relationships.

Skills ACAs develop	*Needed abilities*
Sensitivity to others	Be in touch with own needs
Helpfulness	Set appropriate limits
Able to tune out	Be emotionally present

Contingency planning and re-
  sourcefulness
	Learn to trust one's own percep-
	  tion

Codependency

Children of alcoholics often end up becoming "codependents" of
alcoholic or drug-addicted partners, who "enable" their partner's

substance abuse by making excuses for them, covering up for them, and denying that it's really a problem. ACAs who become codependent have a distorted concept of personal boundaries and have trouble setting limits to unacceptable behavior. They may find a partner whom they can take care of, yet who is not emotionally available. They may put up with abuse and unreliability from their partner, because they don't realize there's anything else they can expect from relating to another person, or because they believe they don't really deserve any better treatment. They may try to control their partner's behavior, because their own life feels so out of control.[11]

When you start taking care of yourself, you become less obsessed with trying to control an alcoholic partner (or one who eats too much, gambles, or engages in any other compulsive behavior). But in order to take care of yourself, you need to know how to set limits.

Setting Limits

A person is more likely to "hit bottom" if other people aren't constantly rescuing him from the consequences of his out-of-control behavior. Being confronted with consequences has the effect of "raising his bottom"—he can no longer count on others to cover for him, and he's forced to deal with how unmanageable his life has become.

If your partner is in denial about his substance abuse, how do you set appropriate limits? You begin by getting support from Al-anon, ACA, or a codependency group. Once you have this support, you'll learn how to take care of yourself, even if your partner refuses to seek help. You can use the following guide to set limits with a partner who is abusing substances.

Clarify What You Want
What is it you want? Do you really want this relationship? Under what conditions? Looking at these issues in your support group, you'll clarify what you want from your partner. Through your own recovery, you realize that you deserve to have an intimate relationship that works for you, and you don't have to put up with abuse, ridicule, or unreliability.

Identify Behaviors You Object To

What are you unwilling to submit yourself to? Being late; not showing up or following through on agreements; requests to cover for him by calling in sick; verbal, sexual, or physical abuse—you need to decide for yourself what your limits are.

Specify Consequences

Depending on your limits, you set the consequence: for example, if he doesn't show up within twenty minutes of the appointed time, you'll leave without him; if he's hung over, you won't call into work for him; if he doesn't follow through on social engagements, you won't make excuses for him; if he hits you, you'll call the police.

Follow Through on Consequences

When you specify consequences, you have to be willing to follow through; otherwise, you simply reinforce his denial. If you're not willing to follow through on a given consequence, you're not ready to set it.

You may wish you could set certain limits and consequences but not feel safe enough to do so because of the threat of physical violence or fears you may have of financial or emotional abandonment. You need to find a way to keep yourself safe—through counseling, getting involved with support groups, finding a job or another place to live. You need to develop enough independence so you're willing to live with the consequences you set. Otherwise, you'll sabotage yourself.

Intervention

A planned confrontation by loved ones, family members, and employers has the potential to break through a person's denial and can be a powerful motivator for seeking treatment. This kind of intervention should be organized with the help of an experienced facilitator, who can meet with everyone involved, so you're prepared to follow through on the consequences you set for him. These might include leaving the relationship, being fired, and cutting off communication unless he goes into treatment.

When You're Both in Recovery

You can easily feel wounded by your partner's mood swings during recovery. He may seem preoccupied and feel irritable. It's hard not to take each other's bad mood personally, especially when one or both partners are also codependent. You may not feel confident that your partner will stay in the relationship once he stops using, or he may respond negatively to the limits you set on unreliable behavior. Likewise, if you stop using, your partner may be confronted with his own substance abuse, or discover that he can no longer use your drinking as an excuse for not pursuing his goals.

In twelve-step programs or similar support groups, you'll see how recovery has affected the lives of other group members, and this will help you anticipate changes in the dynamics of your own relationship. Hearing their stories and telling yours can help you feel good about yourself, even if your partner is having a hard time or there are problems between you. You begin to realize that your partner's annoyance doesn't always have that much to do with you. You can empathize with each other's difficult times, so you're less likely to react negatively to wide-ranging moods.

You don't have to stay isolated and alone. There is a lot of support and help out there for people in recovery. Many gays and lesbians are learning how to live vibrant, fulfilling lives without alcohol or other substances. They're challenging the belief that you have to use some sort of mind-altering substance to have fun or feel good about yourself. Relaxation, massage, dance, meditation, and physical exercise are just some of the ways that more and more people are experiencing a natural high.

Questions and Comments

Q: My partner goes to twelve-step meetings every night of the week. I'm glad he's in recovery, but I feel neglected. It seems to me he has just substituted one crutch for another.

A: Though it's possible that even AA could be used in an addictive manner (if going to meetings interferes with work and relationships, and the rest of your life becomes unmanageable), you may also feel jealous of his program: he meets other men, has great insights, and gets in touch with new and unfamiliar feelings. This process is likely to alter dynamics in your relationship, so it's important to talk to each other about these changes. You could also get some ideas and support for yourself through Al-anon. Tell him you feel neglected, and brainstorm ways to spend time together, while giving each other support for recovery.

Q: My lover won't go to a dinner where wine is served, much less a party with liquor and marijuana. This seems awfully rigid to me—no one's going to force him to drink or use. Besides, I miss him at these events.

A: The recovery process is a matter of life and death. Perhaps later on he'll feel more relaxed around people who are having a glass of wine with dinner, but in the beginning stages of recovery he may need to socialize in clean and sober settings in order to feel supported in his sobriety. Tell him you miss him, and see if you can figure out a way to include him with friends in a setting you both feel comfortable with.

Q: I don't like all the religious references to a "higher power" in AA. If I stop drinking, I want it to be because I've empowered myself.

A: Alcohol use is a problem when you can't predict beforehand whether you'll be able to stop drinking once you start. For an alcoholic, relinquishing the belief that he can control his drinking is the first step to acknowledging that he's powerless over alcohol. For you, the "higher power" might simply be the *recognition* that you don't have control once you start drinking. This knowledge provides you with a good reason not to begin.

Q: I've long been interested in meditation and mystic traditions. I've also read about the ritualized use of drugs in native religions. What exactly is the problem with using chemicals to elicit altered states of consciousness or spiritual awareness?

A: Ritualized use resembles the rules for drinking described in the second phase of "Use versus Abuse," above. As mentioned earlier, cultures that have traditions for the use of certain substances are less likely to abuse the drug.[12]

The main problem with the consistent use of drugs to alter

consciousness is that it reinforces the illusion that drugs are the "cause" of altered states.[13] While drugs may serve as a catalyst, most spiritual traditions demonstrate that profound insights and awareness are just as attainable through nonchemical methods, such as meditation, music, and prayer.[14]

13

Compulsion in Sex and Love

The concept of sexual compulsion wasn't discussed very much in the gay community prior to AIDS. At the beginning of the epidemic, we were encouraged to have safer sex and decrease our sexual contacts. But if we have safe sex, what difference does it make how many men we have sex with? These suggestions appeared to be thinly disguised attempts to encourage us to have monogamous relationships, instead of spreading AIDS. So it's not surprising that gay men would be wary of the recent wave of concern over compulsive sex and romantic addictions.

Yet some gay men feel caught in a cycle of unsatisfying sexual contacts and want to stop the compulsive patterns that leave them emotionally unfulfilled. We can give each other support to recognize and deal with sexual compulsion, while still challenging homophobic and sex-negative attitudes in the surrounding culture.

Sexual Compulsion

Because AIDS has been used as an excuse to stifle sexual exploration, it's important to distinguish what we mean by "sexual compulsion" from arbitrary moral judgments.[1] What defines a compulsion is not so much the specific behavior as how we engage in that behavior. We can do practically anything in a

173

compulsive manner. Compulsive sex doesn't differ a great deal from addictions such as alcohol and substance abuse, or from other compulsions such as eating disorders or working too much.[2] When you decide to go out to eat, stay late at work, have a drink, or make love, you're able to weigh these choices against other interests. But when you feel *compelled* to do any of these things, chances are that you're using these activities to ward off feelings of inadequacy and low self-esteem.

When you subordinate other interests and activities to obtain sexual gratification, you may feel excited at the moment, but you probably won't feel satisfied. Compulsive sex (or any other activity you feel compelled to do) doesn't address your basic need to feel better about yourself. You may obtain some relief through sexual pleasure, yet the furtive nature of the contact makes it unlikely that you'll develop relationships that could help you work through underlying feelings.

Compulsive sex is an attempt to escape from emotional pain. This pain may come from growing up in a dysfunctional family in which you were emotionally, physically, or sexually abused, or it may result from internalized homophobia, social isolation, or major losses. If you never had a relationship with a supportive adult who could listen to you and help you work through these feelings, you may have developed various compulsions to ward them off: alcohol, drugs, overeating, sex or relationship addictions.

Dealing with sexual compulsion is not a question of correcting character defects or responding to moralistic judgments about multiple partners. Recovery from compulsive behavior is a path toward healing from painful feelings, rather than acting out your pain through self-destructive compulsions.

Signs of Sexual Compulsion

When reading through this list, you may be tempted to conclude "No, that's not me." Yet all of us probably use sex in some of the following ways at times. The idea is not so much to define once and for all whether you're a "sex addict," but to consider whether you're using sexual contacts (or even pornography and masturbation) as a way to ward off painful feelings. A person for whom sexual compulsion is a problem may exhibit a number of the following signs.

1. He may have low self-esteem. He may be unaware of having a poor self-image, but he puts himself in dangerous situations by engaging in high-risk behaviors.

2. He lacks confidence in his ability to form intimate relationships. He may be successful in using sex to attract others, but doubts their interest in him emotionally. Some men have a lover but still seek sexual adventures on the side, or use the relationship itself as an addiction.

3. He uses sex to decrease pain. He has a hard time dealing with sadness or conflict. When he feels let down, or other people are making demands on him, he seeks out sex to escape from his feelings.

4. He tends not to discriminate between partners. He may be looking for a certain body type, rather than an actual person, so almost anyone who fits his fantasy image will do.

5. He avoids emotional risks. He tends to remain anonymous, because he's not really interested in getting to know a sexual contact as a real person. Even talking might jolt him out of his fantasy.

6. He loses control over how often he seeks sexual outlets. It no longer feels like a choice; he begins to feel bad if he doesn't keep up a constant stream of sexual contacts or pornography.

7. He doesn't stop when he's satisfied—he can't really be satisfied. He depends on sex for gratification of other needs. He's similar to the person who still feels hungry even when he has had enough to eat: what he's hungry for is emotional sustenance, not food or sex. He can't be satisfied, because he's not really taking care of his underlying emotional needs.

8. He uses sex to increase pleasure. Even when his life is going well, he always wants more; he's never satisfied; it's never enough. It's difficult for him to simply experience his emotions, whether they're painful *or* pleasurable.

9. He subordinates important aspects of his life to his search for sexual contacts. As work and friendships suffer from his neglect, his life becomes increasingly unmanageable.

10. In later stages, even the sexual contact may no longer be pleasurable. Like the addict who loses control in substance abuse, he needs continued sexual contacts simply to prevent the emergence of painful feelings.

In a moment we'll look at how to break through this cycle in order to get at underlying feelings. But first we'll look at how some of these same dynamics play themselves out in compulsive relationships.

Relationship Addiction[3]

Being obsessed with a particular relationship may seem like the opposite of sexual compulsion, but relationship addiction is simply another aspect of compulsive behavior. Some men have one lover, while others have multiple sex partners or masturbate alone, but the same dynamic may be at work: whether through sexual, romantic, or fantasy involvements, the function of the compulsion is to ward off feelings of inadequacy and despair.

Signs of Relationship Addiction

In addition to the characteristics listed above, a person who tends toward relationship addictions exhibits many of the following signs.

1. He may come from a dysfunctional family.[4] His family (and personal) history may include alcohol and substance abuse, incest, or physical violence. Dysfunctional families inhibit the expression of feelings, lower self-esteem, and destroy confidence. Rather than trusting his own feelings and desires, he tends to adapt himself to others' needs.

2. He has few other friends or interests. He's not self-motivated. He doesn't enjoy other interests for their own sake, because he lacks confidence or he's afraid of failure.

3. He is dependent on the relationship for self-esteem. He looks to the relationship to feel good about himself, because he has a hard time feeling good on his own.

4. He is possessive and jealous of his partner's other interests and friends. Rather than welcoming other interests as a stimulating challenge, he sees his partner's interests as a threat, competing for his attention.

5. Neither partner seems improved by their relationship. Rather than attempting an intimate connection, they tend to use each other to fulfill their romantic fantasies. Other friends don't see either partner grow; instead, they seem to drag each other down.

6. He falls into another relationship if someone else happens along. This may seem odd, since he measures his devotion by his depth of feeling—but this "depth" is in response to his fantasy, not the actual person. If he feels neglected, someone else may "sweep him off his feet," and he transfers his feelings to another fantasy object.

7. He's unlikely to remain friends with a former lover. Nothing else was there between them; they didn't really know each other.

8. Following a breakup, he immediately becomes involved with someone else. He can't tolerate grieving for a past relationship, any more than he can tolerate other feelings, so he throws himself into another involvement in order to push those feelings away.

9. He feels threatened by intimate contact. He's not really interested in knowing his partner (or in revealing himself), because this level of intimacy feels too threatening. Despite the drama of jealous scenes, he doesn't really talk about his feelings or solicit feelings from his partner. Intimacy would threaten the facade of his false self.

10. Angry disputes may escalate into violence. What may appear as complete devotion in addictive relationships is really an act of desperation. He attempts to control his partner, even if that means hurting him physically (see the next chapter for a discussion of abusive relationships).

In contrast, a mutually supportive and intimate relationship is characterized by seeing one's partner as a positive choice, rather than clinging to each other out of desperation. Both men want to grow and help the other grow. They're less likely to compete with outside interests for attention. And they want to get to know each other—differences seem stimulating rather than threatening.

* * *

Fear of Intimacy

As mentioned at the end of chapter 5, there's not much point in seeing fear of intimacy as a personality trait. Fear is a feeling, not a character deficit. Addressing the basis of your fear will help you overcome it. What's behind a fear of intimacy? There are two main sources: fear of being too close and fear of emotional abandonment.

Fear of Being Too Close

Some men fear being too close because their parents (or previous lovers) were so intrusive. A mother might have become overinvolved with her son as a substitute for a drunk or emotionally unavailable husband; a father may have tried to guide his son into a career that would have fulfilled his own desires. Both parents might have attempted to live out their own lives through their son by controlling his choices of friends and interests even into young adulthood. At the extreme, they may have invaded his boundaries to the point of incest. He learned that closeness is intrusive and that he won't be able to be himself when he gets too close to someone.

Fear of Abandonment

A man whose parents were intrusive may be wary of being too close, but he may also fear abandonment. Because his parents couldn't tolerate any self-expression that didn't conform to their own needs, he would be abandoned emotionally if he expressed who he really was. As small children we are totally dependent on our parents, so it was better to be intruded upon than abandoned.

Other men fear abandonment not because their parents were too intrusive, but because they were simply not *there.* They may have been preoccupied with an illness in the family, working too hard, drunk, or emotionally unavailable for their son's needs. The child concludes that his parents abandoned him not because of their own problems, but because he was unlovable. As an adult, he still believes there is something essentially wrong with him—that he has to hide who he really is, or he will be "found out" and abandoned, just as his parents abandoned him emotionally.

Because he internalized his parents' incapacity for loving him as he was, he assumes he was unworthy of attention. He believes he must not reveal his thoughts or feelings, because he doesn't trust that anyone will be able to accept him for himself. So he projects an image, and tries to please others in order to prevent abandonment. But because this image is based on a false self, it cannot tolerate much scrutiny. He ends up being abandoned anyway, because he's not really being honest with anyone. So he tries someone else, over and over again.

Recovery

The above cycle can be broken through the process of recovery, which helps you get in touch with feelings, gain insight into the nature of your compulsion, and get the support you need to change your behavior.

Feelings

While working on their recovery from sexual compulsion, men often get in touch with early memories of neglect, emotional abandonment, physical violence, and sexual abuse. For survivors of incest, a pattern of compulsive sexuality may have emerged as a way to gain mastery over the previous trauma. Because of associating sexual activity with shame, you may have sought out sexual contacts in which you continued to be overpowered or degraded. You may get in touch with sorrow and rage for the abuse and emotional abandonment you suffered, as well as guilt and shame for having continued this pattern in your adult life.

Insight

You learn something about how addictions work: compulsive behavior essentially wards off feelings. You learn that your parents' intrusiveness and emotional abandonment were a function of their own emotional incapacity and not a reflection of your self-worth. You also realize that no matter what happened to you as a child, you are now an adult and you have to take responsibility for your own life and recovery.

Stopping the Compulsive Behavior

Some men wish they could continue their compulsive behavior until they feel better about themselves, because they can't imagine giving up sex, alcohol, or other addictions without feeling miserable. But they're unlikely to feel better so long as they're continuing with self-destructive behavior. It becomes more and more difficult to ward off negative feelings as their lives become increasingly unmanageable. They won't be able to heal from their previous hurt until they stop pushing feelings away through compulsive activity.

Getting Support

When you stop compulsive behavior, feelings will emerge and you can begin to deal with them. But this is difficult to do on your own. The emotional (and even physical) pain can feel overwhelming. It's essential that you get support in order to tolerate the feelings that are likely to emerge when you withdraw from compulsive activity. You can get this kind of support through therapy groups focusing on sexual compulsion, or the twelve-step program of Sex and Love Addicts Anonymous.[5]

These groups help you stay in recovery by breaking your isolation. You'll have a safe forum to explore your feelings, where you don't have to put up a front for anyone else. In the beginning, you may think of yourself as different from other group members, but most people eventually find a great deal in common even in mixed groups (men and women, gay and straight). Aside from stopping the behavior, the group encourages you to deal with feelings of remorse and shame. You make amends with whomever it seems appropriate, so you're not simply left with another reason to lower your self-esteem and start the cycle over again.

Recovery from sexual compulsion is *difficult*, even with support. As you get closer to your feelings, you may yearn to act out sexually. Without support, you can end up right back in your old patterns. In addition to SLAA, some men seek out individual therapy, or groups for survivors of incest and other childhood abuse, to deal with the rush of memories and feelings that arise with the cessation of compulsive activity.[6]

*   *   *

Ten Aspects of Healthier Relationships

Recovery from sexual compulsion and relationship addictions enables you to approach sexuality and relationships in the following ways:

1. As you feel better about yourself, you gain confidence in your ability to form intimate relationships.
2. You develop other interests, such as work, community involvement, and friendships.
3. Your attractions develop from a mutual exchange of feelings and a genuine appreciation of the uniqueness of your partner.
4. As sexuality becomes an expression of intimacy and caring, sex becomes a choice rather than a compulsion.
5. You're more likely to take emotional risks, revealing yourself and welcoming feedback from your partner.
6. Both you and your partner feel stimulated by your relationship.
7. You appreciate your partner's interests and other friends.
8. If you have a conflict, you're willing to listen to your partner and consider how you may have contributed to the problem.
9. You're able to hear and understand your partner's feelings without being threatened by them.
10. If your relationship ends, you're still able to see positive qualities in your former partner, understand your own part in the difficulties that led to your separation, and think about what you could do differently in the future.

Through recovery, you're able to get in touch with feelings, rather than warding them off through compulsive sexuality or other addictions. Of course, you don't have to be perfectly "self-actualized" in order to have a relationship. As you reveal more of yourself and learn about your partner, you can help each other work through fears of emotional abandonment and expand your capacity for genuine intimacy.

Questions and Comments

Q: What's wrong with using sex to avoid unpleasant feelings?

A: The effort to keep unpleasant feelings at bay eventually makes the rest of your life unmanageable, and you feel even worse. The problem with using compulsions to evade unpleasant feelings is that in the long run it simply doesn't work. If you realize you're using sex to push away feelings, you don't have to wait until you hit bottom in order to get support.

Though getting in touch with underlying feelings can be painful, you can heal from the grief, sadness, and hurt that you've tried to avoid through compulsive sex, relationship addictions, or drugs. Healing allows the pleasure of having real choices in how you want to live and grow in the world. Sexuality becomes an appealing choice, rather than a desperate craving.

Q: Would you say someone who goes to the baths is sexually compulsive?

A: Sexual compulsion isn't so much a matter where we go to have sex as how we approach sex. The bars and baths lend themselves to casual sex, but having casual sex doesn't necessarily mean you're being compulsive. If you feel compelled to have sex with numerous partners (or even one partner) and you avoid emotionally intimate relationships, it's useful to consider whether your search for sex or romance is an addiction rather than a choice. If you feel bad when you stop, chances are you're using sex to push away feelings.

It's important to remember that you can practice safe sex even if you're still being compulsive. Having safer sex will help you gain control over at least one aspect of your compulsive sexual behavior.

Q: If it weren't for AIDS, I'd still be going to the baths. Isn't all this concern about sexual compulsion just an attempt to reinforce middle-class monogamous norms?

A: Gay men naturally question the motives of people who try to restrict our lifestyles. But some men get stuck in a place where their rebellion against social hypocrisy becomes self-destructive. They want to find other ways to assert themselves and heal from their pain without sacrificing themselves through compulsive behavior.

Q: I can see how I've been compulsive with sex at times, but I don't see how abstinence helps you learn to use sex in healthier ways.

A: Sexuality is a normal expression of intimacy. The idea in recovery from sexual compulsion is not to remain celibate for the rest of your life, but to abstain from sex while you work through your feelings. SLAA suggests having sex only within a committed relationship; you'll have to judge for yourself whether that's a reasonable goal for you.

14

Abusive Relationships

*M*ost couples, despite their mutual caring, end up taking out their frustrations on each other at times. By listening to each other and using assertive messages, you're likely to keep irritable interactions from escalating out of control. But some couples get caught in a vicious circle of abusive retaliation, which they're not able to stop on their own. In this chapter we'll examine the misconceptions and assumptions that underlie violent relationships, and point out steps toward recovery that both partners need to take.

Types of Abuse

Abusive behavior occurs on a continuum from verbal and emotional abuse to destruction of property, sexual assault, and physical violence. When communication has broken down to the extent that arguments often degenerate into shouting matches, sarcasm, and ridicule; if you find yourselves pushing or shoving, throwing things, or threatening to hurt each other; if you've tried to humiliate or control each other sexually; or if you've actually started hitting, it's vitally important that you get some help *now,* to keep these fights from escalating any further.

Emotional Abuse

Emotional (or psychological) abuse can take a variety of forms: sarcasm, put-downs, public humiliation; yelling, intimidation, name-calling; sleep deprivation, blame, and irrational jealousy; destroying property, punching walls, killing pets; and threats of suicide or violence.

Sexual Abuse

Sexual abuse includes oral or anal rape, forced unsafe sex, nonmutual sadomasochism or bondage; unwanted contact with third partners; sex as "duty"; snide remarks about sexual adequacy; sex during physical fights; or any unwanted sexual touching.

Physical Violence

Physical violence tends to escalate in severity and lethality over time: pushing, shaking, poking, slapping, kicking, biting, scratching, pulling hair, hitting with open hand; choking, punching, hitting with closed fists and objects; aimed hitting; and using weapons—sticks, knives, and guns. Of course, even shoving someone can be dangerous, since he can trip and split his skull. Battering relationships can easily escalate to suicide, homicide, or both.

Misconceptions About Violence

Violence is not an intrinsic reflex to frustration. It may have become such a habitual response that it feels like second nature, but violence is *learned*. Since violence is not an automatic response, you can learn other ways to handle frustration.

Violence is commonly depicted in the media as a way to deal with relationship problems, especially for men, but it doesn't solve anything. Violence destroys trust, elicits retaliation, and interferes with your ability (and willingness) to listen to each other. Though a person might have to use force to defend himself from a physical attack, the use of violence to express dissatisfaction in a relationship is an exaggerated response to a misperceived threat.

Profile of the Batterer

A man may have learned to be violent from his own experience: having witnessed violence around him; having to defend himself in previous violent and dangerous situations; and having been physically abused as a child. He may look back on his own abuse as a "good" thing—he thinks it kept him in line, rather than remembering the intense fear and humiliation he felt at the time.

He may have grown up feeling insecure, with low self-esteem. He may pretend to be self-confident and in control, but he feels the discrepancy between the front he presents to the outside world and what he feels inside. He may be quite sensitive but passive. His expectation is that the relationship will help him become all that he has so far pretended to be.

The following list contains some aspects of addictive relationships outlined in the previous chapter, as well as other dynamics that apply especially to batterers:

1. He may have a family (and personal) history of alcohol and substance abuse, incest, or physical violence.
2. He has few other friends or interests.
3. He is dependent on the relationship to feel good about himself.
4. He is possessive and jealous of his partner's other interests and friends.
5. He feels threatened by intimate contact. Despite the drama of jealous scenes, he doesn't really talk about his feelings or solicit feelings from his partner.
6. Angry disputes escalate into violence.
7. In addition to physical abuse and threats of violence, he attempts to control his partner's life through social isolation, emotional put-downs, and sexual abuse.
8. He tends to deny he's being abusive.
9. He minimizes the severity of the abuse.
10. He blames his partner for his own violent acting out.

A phrase commonly used to shift responsibility for the violence to the other person is "If only you hadn't [provoked me, kept whining at me, let me down]." However, no one can *make* someone else be violent. It's his choice to act out his frustration in a violent manner. When he realizes that he's making a choice to be violent, he begins to understand that he has other options, even if he's extremely upset.

Another aspect of addictive relationships that have turned violent is a kind of magical thinking. The batterer thinks his partner should somehow know what he needs and fulfill all his desires. But once we become an adult, another person can't make us like ourselves. Though naturally it feels good when our partner accepts and loves us, our partner's feelings needn't reflect on our own self-worth. The batterer, however, thinks he must compel his partner's love *in order* to feel good about himself. He tends to perceive any move toward independence by his partner as a personal rejection. The slightest deviation from his absolute control feels like a betrayal. If his partner doesn't meet his needs (or what he imagines he needs at the moment), he feels extremely threatened and lashes out.[1]

Profile of the One Who Is Battered

The man who is battered may put up with violence because he was abused as a child, or has such poor self-esteem that he doesn't believe he deserves anything better. He may be socially isolated and lack support from family or friends. He may also be financially dependent on his lover and feel overwhelmed by the thought of being alone. And he continues to hope that if he just tries harder, his partner will stop being violent.

Both men may be addicted to their relationship. The one who is battered may also have the following characteristics:

1. He may have a family (and personal) history of alcohol and substance abuse, incest, or physical violence.
2. He is likely to be codependent (see "Codependency" in chapter 12).
3. He is socially isolated.
4. He is also dependent on the relationship to feel good about himself.
5. He tends to deny that he has been abused.
6. He minimizes the abuse he has experienced.

7. He blames himself for his partner's out-of-control behavior.
8. He has the illusion that he could keep his partner from being violent by trying to "do better."
9. He may think he deserves to be humiliated, threatened, or hit when his partner feels disappointed in him.
10. He doesn't know how to set limits and consequences to his partner's threats, insults, or violence.

Because of these mistaken assumptions, it's not easy for him to reach out for help. In a moment we'll look at some options he has for keeping himself safe. But first let's take a look at the cycle of violence.

The Cycle of Violence

Violence in relationships often follows a predictable cycle: tension builds until one partner strikes out in anger, and then he feels remorseful. But because he hasn't learned another way to deal with his anger, tension builds up again, and the cycle continues. By learning how this cycle operates, you have a better chance of interrupting it. Then you can substitute other methods for resolving conflicts that are likely to help your relationship grow, rather than damage it.

Tensions Build
A man who has become violent is often not as in touch with his feelings as he thinks. He may let irritations build without realizing how angry he is; then all it takes for him to lash out is feeling slighted by his partner.

Violence Occurs
A man may claim the "insanity defense"—a rage came over him, and he "couldn't help himself." But violence is a *decision*. The decision to become violent takes place in three rapid-fire stages:[2]

1. He *decides* to depersonalize his boyfriend ("no-good lousy bastard").
2. He *decides* to go after him.
3. He *decides* to hit him.

Understanding that he *decides* to be violent, he realizes that he has control over his violence. He doesn't have to be violent when he feels threatened. He can learn other ways to handle his frustration.

Remorse
After he's violent, he may feel sorry and shower his boyfriend with attention. They may feel very close, and have the most passionate sex ever. His partner may believe him when he promises it will never happen again. It's not that he's lying; he may mean it at the time. But this "hearts and flowers" period never lasts. Something always happens to disappoint him, and unless he has learned another way of handling his frustration, he's likely to be violent again.

Breaking the Cycle—Taking Responsibility

Many men don't justify their violence; they feel genuinely ashamed. But feeling ashamed is not sufficient to stop the violence. Unless he confronts his own feelings, he will continue to see the source of contentment outside of himself. If he doesn't learn other ways of dealing with his frustration, he will continue to use violence to express his pain.

The first step in stopping violent behavior is to realize that he's responsible for his own violence. How his partner acts doesn't *make* him violent. If he doesn't like what his partner is doing, he can identify the behavior he objects to and say how he feels about it. He can listen to his partner and then negotiate some agreements. If none of this works, he can set limits to their interaction by leaving the scene and by insisting that they get some professional help. If his partner isn't willing to work on problems, he doesn't have to stay in the relationship. He has options for dealing with conflict, apart from violence.

Another way of breaking the cycle is if his *partner* realizes he doesn't have to put up with violence. He may leave the relationship, move out, or at least stay with a friend. He can insist that they both get help so they can learn to deal with their problems without resorting to violence.

Mutual battering also takes place, and this may be more

common in same-sex couples than in heterosexual relationships.[3] The power dynamics are different in mutual battering, but it can be just as destructive, perhaps more so. The danger of escalation is even greater. This is an extremely serious problem, with life-threatening implications. And without professional help, it's likely to get worse.

Seeking Assistance for Battering Relationships

It would be a disservice in a self-help book to suggest that you'll be able to interrupt the cycle of violence on your own. It is essential to get professional assistance for domestic violence. Help is available in groups, both for men who batter and for men who are battered. If there are no groups available where you live, you can get help from a therapist who has experience with domestic violence.

Seeking Help for the One Who Is Battered
You need to feel empowered to take care of yourself. You may be reluctant to admit you've been battered, especially since reaching out challenges the closed system in which violence occurs, and you may fear reprisal. It's possible to learn how to set limits and consequences to your partner's behavior and follow through on them. For the reasons outlined above, this may be difficult to do on your own.

In some cities, there are groups for battered men where you can talk with others who have been able to get out of similar situations.[4] A group (or a therapist familiar with domestic violence) can counter your isolation, educate you about the dynamics of battering, and help you think clearly about your choices:

1. You can't keep your partner from being violent by trying to "do better."
2. You can't predict when your partner will be violent.
3. You're *not* responsible for getting hit.
4. You *don't* deserve to be humiliated, threatened, or hit when your partner is disappointed in you (or even if you're disappointed in yourself).
5. You're not responsible for how your partner feels about himself.

6. You can recognize and acknowledge the severity of the abuse.
7. You can set limits, with consequences, to your partner's behavior.
8. You deserve to have a relationship in which you have no fear of being assaulted.
9. You can learn where to go if you need a safe place.
10. You can learn how to get a temporary restraining order, and how to deal with the criminal justice system if you decide to press charges.

Though you're not responsible for your partner's violence, you *are* responsible for deciding whether to stay in an abusive relationship. Other men in your support group may challenge your decision to stay with your partner, especially if he refuses treatment. Reaching out to others for support can help you feel less threatened by the possibility of leaving the relationship, if that's what it takes to keep yourself safe.

You may be reluctant to set limits and consequences out of fear of retaliation, or that you'll get your partner in "trouble." But you're not doing him any favor by protecting him from the consequences of his out-of-control behavior. Your efforts can provide help for both of you—when you seek support for yourself, he may also get the help he needs.

Seeking Help for the Batterer

It's hard to admit that you've been hitting the man you love most in the world. Remember how you felt following the latest battering incident? Don't just promise to do better; use your resolve to get some help.

Battering is best dealt with in a group with other batterers. In the group, the men challenge one another's denial, minimization, and blame. They counter unrealistic beliefs about what a relationship should provide. The group breaks your isolation and creates a support system in which you can try out new skills and gain the confidence you need in order to put them into practice.

Groups specifically for gay men who batter are now available in some cities.[5] Though some of the dynamics may differ from heterosexual battering situations, there are enough similarities that joining a group for straight men could be worthwhile if there aren't any gay groups available in your area (assuming, of course, that you let the facilitators know you're gay and the other men are able to deal with that difference in the group). If no group is available anywhere near you, then at least find a therapist who has experience working with domestic violence. If you've also been drinking or using drugs, you need to stop (see chapter 12).

Most therapists won't do couples therapy unless the violence has ended and the batterer (or both partners, in the case of mutual battering) has already gotten the support he needs from a group to learn other ways to deal with his frustration. The reason for insisting on separate therapy for couples who batter is that the process of couples therapy can be stressful. Both partners must feel confident that they will work through their difficulties, rather than acting out their distress through violence. If one partner is fearful about what will happen to him once they get home, he's unlikely to say what's really bothering him. Despite the best of intentions, a pattern of coercion will continue unless it has already been dealt with, and this will undermine the therapy. It is dangerous to add to their stress without having provided the resources for them to stop the violent behavior.

Ten Techniques for Handling Anger

Feeling angry doesn't *cause* violence, but someone who has been out of control needs to learn other ways to handle his anger. Among other skills in a group of batterers, you'll learn how to:

1. Monitor your irritation level
2. Identify primary feelings
3. Identify triggering events
4. Counter irrational beliefs
5. Practice positive self-talk
6. Express your needs assertively
7. Recognize escalating behaviors
8. Practice relaxation exercises
9. Use time-outs to de-escalate conflict
10. Reach out to others

1. Monitor Your Irritation Level

You monitor your irritation level on a scale of one to ten at various times throughout the day, but especially following any upsetting incidents. Some men don't want to get in touch with feelings because they fear becoming violent again. Yet if you recognize when you feel irritated, you're less likely to let the anger build up until you're enraged.

2. Identify Primary Feelings

Men are socialized to think that anger is the only emotion it's all right for us to be in touch with or express. Anger may really be an expression of hurt, frustration, inadequacy, or fear of rejection. You begin to identify primary feelings of sadness, hurt, and fear. Instead of lashing out when you're angry, you realize "I'm really mad—that must mean I feel hurt, sad, or afraid. What's the behavior I'm upset about, and how do I really feel?"

3. Identify Triggering Events

You learn to identify events that trigger your feelings: opposition, disappointment, frustration, and your own irrational assumptions.

4. Counter Irrational Beliefs

You learn how to counter mistaken notions that your lover should be able to know what you want at any moment and provide it for you. You begin to counter your sense of "entitlement," which contributes to feelings of impotence and rage if you don't get what you want.

5. Practice Positive Self-talk

You affirm to yourself that you can handle tough situations:

"I don't need to escalate just because my partner opposes me."

"Don't jump to the worst conclusions—what is he really trying to tell me?"

"I don't have to be totally on top of everything—it's okay to be confused or unsure of myself."

"If things get too hard, I can call a time-out."

6. Express Your Needs Assertively

In place of violence, you learn how to express yourself assertively. Rather than letting irritations build up until you explode, you identify the behavior you're upset about. Then you can say how you feel, without blaming or threatening your partner. Identifying behaviors and feelings helps you negotiate a solution that takes both of you into consideration.

7. Recognize Escalating Behaviors

The group helps you reconstruct violent incidents, and you learn how to recognize signs that indicate you're beginning to lose control—for example, you notice you're sweating or trembling; you raise your voice and interrupt your partner; or you make threatening gestures.

8. Practice Relaxation Exercises

By learning how to relax, you feel less tense and anxious, and this will help you think more clearly. One exercise consists of tensing and relaxing each part of your body, from your feet to your head. Another is to take a deep breath and let it out slowly, allowing all parts of your body to relax. You repeat this a dozen times.

9. Use Time-Outs to De-Escalate Conflict[6]

Time-outs are used to defuse a tense situation. It's important for both partners to understand the ground rules, so that neither of you experiences the time-out as an unfair abandonment. If you sense that you're in danger of escalating out of control, you call "Time out." Or your partner can call "Time out" if he feels unsafe. You must leave the scene without arguing.

A time-out consists of telling your partner that you're leaving for an hour. During this time you agree not to drive, drink, or destroy property. If there is no other phone within walking distance, don't drive any further than necessary to reach a phone. You call another group member, who helps you identify your primary feelings, practice relaxation exercises, and go over your list of positive self-talk.

Then you come home, and you try again to discuss the topic, sticking to behaviors and feelings. If you escalate again, you take another time-out.

10. Reach Out to Others

Most men in abusive relationships are socially isolated. By reaching out in the group, you increase social contacts, ventilate pent-up feelings, and get feedback about your behavior and perceptions.

You don't have to endure violence in your relationship. Help is available for men who are battered: you can learn how to take care of yourself and set limits to unacceptable behavior. Help is also available for men who batter: you can learn to express feelings without becoming violent. And you can both reach out for support to feel better about yourselves in the process of recovery from a violent relationship.

Questions and Comments

Q: How do you tell if you're being battered?

A: If you're being ridiculed, threatened, or touched in a way you don't like, and your partner doesn't stop when you tell him to (or you're afraid to set limits with him), then you're being emotionally, sexually, or physically battered.

Q: I don't like it when my partner puts me down or hits me, but when I balance it against the rest of the relationship, I guess I'm willing to put up with it. I know he's never going to change.

A: Many people think the hearts-and-flowers stage is the only part of your relationship that's "real," and the abuse is simply what you have to put up with in order to get to the part that feels good. You may not be willing to say anything for fear it will lead to another fight. But by not setting limits, you're rescuing him from having to deal with the consequences of his behavior.

While many relationships end once the violence is confronted, some couples are able to reach a new equilibrium without violence—but only if *both* men seek treatment. You may be afraid to rock the boat, but chances are the violence will get worse. Therapy could help you learn how to keep yourself safe, and clarify whether this abuse is really what you're willing to settle for. You deserve better.

Q: Doesn't drinking cause violence?

A: Alcohol doesn't *cause* violence, but it does lower inhibitions. A man who has learned to use violence to express his frustration may use drinking as an excuse for his violence. While it's vital for men in abusive relationships to stop drinking, they must also learn other ways to handle their frustrations.

Q: Can't someone provoke violence?

A: The person who gets hit isn't necessarily an angel. Both partners no doubt contribute to the difficulties they have in communicating their hurt. Verbal abuse can provoke a very negative response, for example, but each person is responsible for how he chooses to react. He can say how he feels, call a time-out, say he wants to go into counseling, or even leave the relationship. He has choices; no one can really "make" someone be violent.

15

What If It Doesn't Work Out?

Maintaining a gay relationship in a homophobic society can be difficult. We don't have the institution of marriage, help from families, or recognition from the surrounding culture that our relationships are important. Lacking positive models and emotional support, you can feel isolated with your problems. But the issues you're confronting with your partner may be common to other couples. They can help you gain some perspective on your conflicts to determine whether you're really incompatible or if you're feeling overwhelmed by outside pressures.

Let's assume you've gotten outside support and sorted through your conflicts to see which ones derive from homophobic social pressures and which arise from your own relationship; you've used the listening and conflict-resolution skills outlined here, and even sought professional help—yet it still appears that you're incompatible. Now what?

As your lives intertwined, you began to expect that your relationship would continue. Unraveling can be very painful, even if both partners realize it's not working for them. If one partner decides to leave while the other still hopes to make a go of it, it's even more difficult. You may end up feeling hurt, guilt, anger, and resentment. A lack of trust can make it difficult to talk with your partner about your feelings. But it's easier to reach a sense of closure if you're able to empathize with each other about the end of your relationship.

Practical Decisions

It helps if, when you first combined resources, you made an agreement about how to separate your financial involvements and divide common property should you ever split up.[1] Obviously, no one likes to think about how the relationship will end when you're first getting together, but these agreements can help you separate without using financial disputes to express resentments. Couples counseling can also help you sort through your feelings, and provide a safe place to take care of practical issues if you decide to end your relationship.

Though some men prefer to put off these negotiations until they feel calmer about the separation, wrapping things up can be an important part of reaching closure.

Adjusting to the Loss

While many gay men maintain close friendships with former lovers, this transition can take a while. When you've just separated, it can be extremely painful to be around each other, especially if the ending wasn't mutual or if your partner has already gotten involved with someone else. You may need some time apart for a few months to mourn for the loss of the relationship, heal from your hurt and disappointment, and nurture your self-esteem.

Mourning resembles the response to life-threatening illness described in chapter 10.

Denial

If it was not a mutual decision to end the relationship, there's often a state of shock, denial, or disbelief—how can this really be happening? You thought everything was going fine, and you find out he's not satisfied or he has found someone else. This can be such a blow to your confidence and self-esteem that you begin to doubt your perception in other areas of your life.

Bargaining
You may try to hold the relationship together by giving in on previous disputes, or trying a last-ditch effort at couples counseling.

Anger
You may feel angry and betrayed. If he has left you for someone else, his current happiness may seem hopelessly unfair. Since he may not be available to empathize with your feelings, you'll need to reach out to other friends, who can listen to your disappointment and appreciate the depth of your hurt and anger.

Depression
Once it sinks in that a significant part of your life is gone, you may feel depressed and listless, previous interests pale in their importance, and you figure what's the use in trying anything.

Acceptance
You finally resign yourself that you're really single again. After a while, you begin to notice that you have a little more energy for other interests, and begin to adjust to life as a single person.

Unfinished Grief

Sometimes people aren't able to work all the way through the loss of a relationship. Following are three common ways that you might get stuck, and some ideas for helping yourself move on.

Cynicism
You may try to protect yourself from further disappointment by developing a disdainful or cynical attitude toward relationships. Cynicism wards off the current pain, and protects you from getting hurt in the future, but in the long run it will keep you isolated. Cynicism is a sign that you haven't yet healed from past hurt. If you allow yourself to grieve for the loss, you'll eventually be able to open yourself to the possibility of a new relationship.

On the Rebound
Another way to avoid the intensity of the grieving process is to throw yourself into another relationship. A new boyfriend will

distract you from your grief, but if you haven't allowed yourself to grieve for your recent loss, you may not be using the best judgment in your next relationship choice.

Comparisons

When you meet someone new, comparisons are only natural. You can't help but notice similarities and differences. Being with someone new will never feel quite the same, because each person is unique and every relationship has its own dynamic. You may fear that no one will ever measure up to your former lover (or you expect a new partner to abandon you). But it is possible, over time, to develop depth with another man. As you get to know each other, you appreciate the growth of your own relationship, rather than constantly comparing him with others from your past.

Countering Negative Thinking

The dissolution of a long-term relationship can be a major blow to your self-esteem, triggering doubts and insecurities. You may internalize the rejection, wondering if there's something wrong with you, and you may feel pessimistic about ever finding anyone who really wants to be with you. Though you may think about what else you might have tried to make the relationship work, it's a mistake to assume that your former lover's lack of interest means you're not worthy of an intimate relationship.

There's no reason to talk yourself out of feeling sad—sadness is a natural response to disappointment and loss. Allowing yourself to cry and feel the depth of your hurt enables you to heal from the pain of your loss. It's possible to feel disappointed without jumping to negative conclusions about your own self-worth.

Affirmations can be used to counter negative thinking: "I *am* worthwhile; I'm a lovable human being; I have many good qualities. I'm really sad, but that doesn't mean I'm not a good person or that I'll never find anyone else." Becoming immobilized for a time is only natural, but after a while it helps to reach out to friends and keep up with former interests.

Loneliness

Loneliness has a negative connotation in our culture. Images of the lovelorn pining away feed into our fears of desperation. We tend to see loneliness as a character deficit, rather than a natural reaction to emotional deprivation, and blame ourselves for feeling lonely. This, of course, only lowers our self-esteem and makes it even more difficult to reach out to others.

Recent studies confirm many people's subjective experience that a lack of emotional involvement results in distress, tension, restlessness, anxiety, and even impaired immune functioning.[2] The feelings of acute longing following the loss of a lover are exacerbated by social isolation. Gay men who are separated (or alienated) from their families, new in town, and lacking a larger support network are particularly vulnerable to loss.

We feel our isolation more keenly during holidays (or even Saturday nights), when others are celebrating the emotional connections we lack. Social isolation can also lead to seeing others as being aloof.[3] This may explain our tendency to perceive gay men as having "attitude" in bars, where other men are probably just as shy and vulnerable as we are.

Gay men may feel the loss of a relationship even more keenly than heterosexuals, if we're isolated and lack supportive friends. Just as hunger is a natural response to going without food, pangs of loneliness are a natural response to emotional deprivation. Loneliness is nothing to be ashamed of. It's a signal that we lack involvement with a significant person in our lives and it's time to reach out.

Moving On

You may still miss the companionship, even if you think it was the right decision to end your relationship. Gradually, as you discover your own rhythms and spend time with friends, you may even find that you enjoy being alone, getting to know yourself. Released from whatever compromises you made in your past relationship, you begin to reassess your priorities and think of other projects, work, or where else you'd like to live.

If you're left in the home you shared with your partner, you may want to change things around to make it yours again—paint, rearrange the furniture, remove certain objects that remind you too strongly of your former lover. Making a clean sweep can be a symbolic way of beginning anew. You may want to store some things for a while and decide later what to do with them.

Eventually you may feel it's time to start dating again. After a long relationship, the whole dating scene can be intimidating. Times have changed since the onset of AIDS; you may not be interested anymore in one-night stands (or maybe right now that's *all* you're interested in), and you've never had to negotiate safe sex before.

Some people say you can't really look for a lover; he'll simply come along when you're ready, at the most unexpected time. While a certain degree of readiness certainly helps, there are some things you can do to increase your chances of meeting men who are available.[4]

Let friends know you're back in circulation, and go out with single friends. Consider activities you neglected for a while because your former lover wasn't interested in them. Check calendars in gay papers for activities or classes, and look through the personal ads to see if there are others who share your interests. Expand your social network by getting to know a number of men. Making new friends is a good way to meet someone you'll eventually feel closer to. Be yourself, follow your intuition, and see what develops!

Questions and Comments

Q: Do you need a lover to be happy?

A: Though it's not necessary to be in a primary love relation-ship to have a fulfilling life, we do need emotional ties and a sense of belonging. Some people value their solitude and are content with being single, but a real appreciation for the richness of solitude arises, for the most part, from a foundation of deep emotional involvement. Close friendships, meaningful work, and community interests can all provide a sense of emotional connec-tion and well-being, even if you don't have a primary love rela-tionship.

Q: All of these suggestions sound good to me, but nothing seems to work. Since my lover left I've been so miserable I could just die.

A: After splitting up, some people become so depressed that

they're not able to remobilize themselves. Self-help books can provide some useful ideas, but their suggestions require that you have enough energy to follow through on them, and when you're severely depressed you may not have the wherewithal to counter negative thinking, much less reach out to friends or expand your social network. If you're not able to get moving again on your own, psychotherapy can provide the support you'll need to handle your grief. Call your community mental health services, or ask around for private referrals.

Q: Are there certain signs that it's a good idea to leave a relationship?

A: We've discussed a number of signs that a relationship needs help (see chapters 11 and 14), but the decision to leave is a very personal one. If you've tried to negotiate solutions to your conflicts and used couples counseling to explore how you both contribute to your difficulties, and you still think you're incompatible, you may want to consider separating and see how you both feel.

If your partner batters you and refuses to get help, you should definitely leave and get a restraining order. If your partner is abusing alcohol or drugs and refuses to get help, get support for yourself so you can learn how to set limits and figure out whether it's worth it for you to stay.

Q: A couple I've spent a lot of time with just split up. I like them both, but they're very angry with each other. I'd like to spend time with each of them, but I don't want to take sides.

A: It's hard on friends when lovers split up. Whose friends are whose? You feel a divided loyalty. When you spend time with each friend, you can reflect his feelings without taking sides. But if hearing their anger toward each other feels too uncomfortable, you can suggest that they talk about their feelings with other friends, who aren't as close to both of them.

Q: When I broke up with my lover I said I'd still like to be friends, but he said he doesn't trust me anymore.

A: He needs to grieve for the loss of your relationship, and it may take a while before he's ready to consider being friends. You might try checking in with him in a few weeks to see if he'd like to get together to talk about feelings left over from your breakup. See if you can empathize with what it was like for him to be rejected, even if you don't think you were at fault. Feeling heard and understood may enable him to reconsider whether he wants to be friends with you.

EPILOGUE

This book provides some ideas for handling conflicts that are likely to arise in gay relationships. These strategies are applicable to many other areas we have scarcely touched on, such as differences in age, class, or ethnic backgrounds, dealing with disability, later stages of development, buying a house, or where to spend your next vacation.

When you feel confident about your ability to resolve conflicts, you can be more spontaneous and develop your own shortcuts for handling disagreements. Chances are you're not as likely to be furious with each other when you keep on top of issues as they develop, and you can give fuller vent to your feelings without being afraid your conflict will escalate out of control. If you become too upset to listen, you can let your partner know you feel defensive; if your conflict degenerates into a quarrel, you can come back again later to talk about your feelings, once you've cooled down.

Developing Intimacy

As mentioned earlier, intimacy is not just a matter of shared interests and sexual compatibility. Intimacy grows out of our willingness to talk about the major and minor issues in our lives, including how we feel toward each other. Following are a few ideas for keeping in touch as your relationship develops.

Reveal yourself

Let each other know what you think and how you feel. You can allow each other to feel sad, frustrated, or disappointed without assuming that the other is responsible, or that there's necessarily a problem to solve. Tell your partner when you want some attention and when you'd prefer to spend some time by yourself.

Ask About Him

Sometimes we're so preoccupied with ourselves that we forget to ask about what's going on with the other person. Remember your partner: solicit his opinion, ask how he's feeling, and listen to his responses.

Tell Him What You Appreciate About Him

Naturally you're cautious about coming on too strong. You both need to believe your feelings are really in response to each other—that you're not simply "in love with love." By identifying what he does or says that you like or admire, your appreciations are grounded in reality, so they're less likely to be experienced as idle flattery.

Check Out Your Assumptions

You might like to anticipate his needs, but you can't be expected to read each other's minds. If he's had a hard day or some bad news and you're not sure if he wants comforting or to be left alone, ask.

Don't Pigeonhole

Avoid "always" and "never." They're rarely true, and tend to box us in. You might be willing to try all kinds of things occasionally—surprise him. (Surprise yourself!)

Don't Just Be Bored; Talk About It

You may think you should never be bored in your relationship, and if you are you should keep it to yourself. So you end up avoiding each other instead. But rather than acting out your boredom by withdrawing, talk about it. Don't blame your partner for being boring; just say you're bored. If you're bored, he could very well be too. Use boredom to help you get in touch with how you really feel, and figure out what else you'd like to do.

Deal with Issues as They Arise

No one wants to be nit-picked, but it's also important not to pile up resentments and then resort to ultimatums. Don't build cases against each other or hold grudges. Take one issue at a time and deal with it.

Don't Hide Your Preference Behind a Question

People often use questions as an invitation: "Would you like something to eat?" or "Would you like to spend the night?" This seems like a harmless convention, but sometimes people will ask a question to hint at their own desires: you're hiking up a long hill and your partner says "Aren't you tired?" when what he really means is "I'm tired and I'd like to rest." Many questions can be restated as your own thoughts or preference. You often reveal more about yourself when you make statements instead of asking questions.

Don't Second-guess Your Partner

Be aware of unspoken accommodations. Don't "rescue" your partner by saying you want to do something when you don't—you'll only end up resenting him later. You can acknowledge your partner's needs without necessarily being able to meet them. Say what you want, and if you want different things, negotiate a solution that takes you both into consideration.

Develop Your Sense of Humor

A sense of humor and playfulness will help you maintain a perspective on problems in your relationship. Humor can also be used in a hostile manner; see if you can laugh at yourselves at least as much as you tease each other.

Intimacy develops from the freedom to reveal ourselves: our sorrows, fears, and hesitations; our thoughts, desires, and dreams. When your partner knows and loves who you really are, it can be a relief not to hide your feelings from each other, or from yourself. Affirming a sense of wholeness within ourselves allows us to explore the depths of love and intimacy with another man.

NOTES AND REFERENCES

Chapter 1

1. "Disclosure Output and Input in College Students," by S. M. Jourard and P. Richman, *Merrill-Palmer Quarterly of Behavior Development* 9 (1963): 141–48.

Male couples, however, tend to communicate more about *sex* than heterosexual couples do. *Homosexuality in Perspective,* by William Masters and Virginia Johnson (Boston: Little, Brown and Company, 1979), pp. 212–21. It would be interesting to know whether gay men talk as much about feelings.

2. *The Male Couple—How Relationships Develop,* by David P. McWhirter and Andrew M. Mattison (Englewood Cliffs, N.J.: Prentice-Hall, 1984), p. 16. McWhirter and Mattison identify various stages couples have experienced in their relationships. These stages were derived from the male couples in their study—they are not intended to prescribe how our own relationships should develop. But it can be reassuring to see that others have gone through some of the same struggles we find ourselves confronted with.

Chapter 2

1. The term "reflection of feelings" was used by Carl Rogers at Ohio State University in his research on the use of empathy in psychotherapy. See *A Way of Being,* by Carl Rogers (Boston: Houghton Mifflin, 1980), p. 138.

Rogers originally identified warmth, empathy, and genuineness as essential qualities for therapeutic change in "The Necessary and Sufficient Conditions of Therapeutic Personality Change," *Journal of Consulting Psychology* 21 (1957): 95–103. These qualities are really the basis for developing intimacy in any relationship: you help your partner get in touch with his feelings when you express your concern for him (warmth), when you understand and can identify with his feelings (empathy), and when you're willing to reveal your own hopes and desires (genuineness).

Chapter 3

1. Behavior, effects, and feelings are identified as the essential components of an "I" message in Thomas Gordon's Effectiveness Training series. See *Leadership Effectiveness Training,* by Thomas Gordon (New York: Wyden Books, 1977), p. 101.

Chapter 4

1. While acknowledging that gay men often encounter communication difficulties, especially in later stages of their relationships, McWhirter and Mattison suggest that gay couples have a tendency to "over-communicate": "At times they process their feelings and behaviors 'to the death,' causing relationship fatigue and distress." "Psychotherapy for Gay Male Couples," by David P. McWhirter and Andrew M. Mattison, in *Gay Relationships,* edited by John P. De Cecco (New York: Haworth Press, 1988), p. 253. The quality of our communication may be more important than the quantity.

Chapter 5

1. The concept of projective identification was introduced by Melanie Klein in "Notes on Some Schizoid Mechanisms," *International Journal of Psychoanalysis,* Volume 27, Part 3, 1946. This concept has been further developed by object relations theorists.

2. *Projective Identification and Psychotherapeutic Technique,* by Thomas H. Ogden (New York: Jason Aronson, 1982), pp. 36–37.

3. See *After the Honeymoon—How Conflict Can Improve Your Relationship,* by Daniel B. Wile (New York: John Wiley and Sons, 1988), p. 212. Wile demonstrates how talking *about* the pattern can help you avoid simply acting it out.

Chapter 6

1. See *Lesbian Couples,* by D. Merilee Clunis and G. Dorsey Green (Seattle: Seal Press, 1988). This book has a number of examples dealing with class, age, and ethnic differences and disability in relationships.

2. *Gay Couples,* by Joseph Harry (New York: Praeger, 1984), pp. 80–81. In Harry's study, the relationships of male couples who didn't live together were just as rewarding as those of couples who did. The main difference was that couples who lived together expected a greater expression of feelings and affection, while those who lived separately were satisfied with less emotional commitment.

Other resources: *Legal Guide for Lesbian and Gay Male Couples,* by Hayden Curry and Denis Clifford (Berkeley: Nolo Press, 1989), has sample contracts for working through financial agreements when you decide to live together.

The Male Couple's Guide to Living Together—What Gay Men Should Know about Living Together and Coping in a Straight World, by Eric Marcus (New York: Harper and Row, 1988). This book includes suggestions for handling money, insurance, and wills, buying property, and moving in together. His interviews with male couples describe how they have dealt with numerous issues in their relationships.

Permanent Partners—Building Gay and Lesbian Relationships That Last, by Betty Berzon (New York: E. P. Dutton, 1988), has a chapter on legal protections for gay relationships. In addition to suggestions for improving our relationships, she discusses the role of money in understanding power dynamics.

Chapter 7

1. *The Male Couple,* p. 94.
2. Ibid.
3. *Male Sexuality,* by Bernie Zilbergeld (New York: Bantam, 1981), p. 332.
4. The San Francisco AIDS Foundation, among others, sponsors "Hot and Healthy Sex" workshops.
5. Derived from San Francisco AIDS Foundation guidelines and suggestions from the Gay Men's Health Collective, New York.
6. Recommended by the San Francisco AIDS Foundation.
7. For example, AZT is being prescribed for men who are antibody positive and whose T-cells are less than 200 but who are otherwise asymptomatic. Pentamidine is also being used to prevent pneumocystis in men who have not been diagnosed with AIDS.
8. For further discussion of the medical causes of impotence, see *The New Sex Therapy: Active Treatment of Sexual Dysfunction,* by H. S. Kaplan (New York: Brunner/Mazel, 1974).
9. *Men's Health* (September 1988): 9. This issue contains a list of medications that can cause impotence and describes treatments for physiologically based erection difficulties.
10. For a description of the squeeze technique and other approaches to sexual dysfunction, see *Human Sexual Inadequacy,* by W. H. Masters and V. E. Johnson (Boston: Little Brown and Co., 1970).
11. *The Tao of Love and Sex,* by Jolan Chang (New York: E. P. Dutton, 1977), p. 42.
12. See *Sexual Consequences of Disability,* edited by Alex Comfort (New York: D. Van Nostrand Co., 1978).

For a selected annotated bibliography on sexuality and disability, write the Sex Information and Education Council of the U.S., 84 Fifth Avenue, New York, New York 10011.

For other suggestions on gay sexual expression, see *The Joy of Gay Sex: An Intimate Guide for Gay Men to the Pleasures of a Gay Lifestyle,* by Dr. Charles Silverstein and Edmund White (New York: Pocket Books, 1986), and *Men Loving Men: A Gay Sex Guide and Consciousness Book,* by Mitch Walker (San Francisco: Gay Sunshine Press, 1985).

Chapter 8

1. See *Man to Man—Gay Couples in America,* by Charles Silverstein (New York: Morrow and Company, 1981), p. 113, for a discussion of "excitement seekers" and "nest builders."
2. *The Male Couple,* p. 5. In McWhirter and Mattison's study, for example, though many couples originally intended their relationships to be sexually exclusive, only 7 out of 156 couples remained consistently monogamous.

3. See *Gay Couples,* p. 140. Harry's research suggests that couples who communicate well are likely to work through differences over sexual exclusivity.

4. *Sexual Behavior in the Human Male,* by A. Kinsey, W. Pomeroy, and C. Martin (Philadelphia: Saunders, 1948), p. 650.

Chapter 9

1. Parents and Friends of Lesbians and Gays is an organization that provides support groups in which parents can talk about their own coming-out process as parents of a gay son or a lesbian daughter. They have chapters in most urban areas. Contact Federation of Parents and Friends of Lesbians and Gays, P. O. Box 24565, Los Angeles, Calif. 90024.

A good book for parents is *Now That You Know: What Every Parent Should Know About Homosexuality,* by Betty Fairchild and Nancy Hayward (New York: Harvest/HBJ, 1979).

2. See *Beyond Acceptance—Parents of Lesbians and Gays Talk about Their Experiences,* by Carolyn Welch Griffin, Marian J. Wirth, and Arthur G. Wirth (Englewood Cliffs, N.J.: Prentice-Hall, 1986).

3. For a discussion of various parenting options, such as coparenting, adoption, foster care, and artificial insemination, see *Gay Parenting—A Complete Guide for Gay Men and Lesbians with Children,* by Joy Schulenburg (Garden City, N.Y.: Anchor Press/Doubleday, 1985).

4. See *The Last Closet: A Gay Parents' Guide for Coming Out to Your Children,* by Andre "Rip" Corley (Pompano Beach, FL: Exposition University, 1988), and *Whose Child Cries—Children of Gay Parents Talk About Their Lives,* by Joe Gantz (Rolling Hills, CA: Jalmar Press, 1983).

5. See *Gay Couples,* p. 143. Harry's study suggests that gay friends help to "legitimize the relationships of gay couples." In addition, "Having gay friends was also found to inhibit any decline in emotional intimacy with age."

6. For a discussion of the legal implications of coparenting agreements, see the *Legal Guide for Lesbian and Gay Male Couples.*

Chapter 10

1. *On Death and Dying,* by Elizabeth Kübler-Ross (New York: Macmillan, 1970). The order of these stages naturally varies from person to person.

2. "Emotion-Immunity Link in HIV Infection," *Science News* 134 (August 20, 1988): 116. This article reports on research conducted by Nancy T. Blaney of the University of Miami School of Medicine, presented at the American Psychological Association's annual meeting in Atlanta, August 1988.

3. Ibid. This article also cites a study by Mary Ann Fletcher of the University of Miami, which showed improved immune functioning in HIV-positive men who participated in a ten-week exercise group.

In a study by Lydia Temoshok of the University of California, San Francisco, exercise was correlated with increased natural killer cell activity. In addition, higher numbers of T-cell subsets were found among people with AIDS who were assertive and who had lower levels of tension, depression, and stress. Paper presented at the American Association for the Advancement of Science, San Francisco, January 1988.

4. *Legal Guide,* p. 205.

5. From a study on psychoneuroimmunology in persons with AIDS by Dr. George F. Solomon, University of California, Los Angeles, reported in *Parade Magazine,* September 18, 1988.

6. *Stragegies for Survival: A Gay Men's Health Manual for the Age of AIDS,* by Martin Delaney and Peter Goldblum (New York: St. Martin's Press, 1987), p. 277.

7. See *Illness as Metaphor,* by Susan Sontag (New York: Vintage Books, 1979). She describes how early in this century tuberculosis was associated with a romantic death wish, and how even today some people associate cancer with certain personality types. Her thesis is that once we understand the nature of a disease, we're less likely to see the illness as a metaphor for psychological problems. Her most recent work is *AIDS and Its Metaphors* (New York: Farrar, Straus and Giroux, 1988).

8. See *The Quilt: Stories from the NAMES Project,* by Cindy Ruskin, photographs by Matt Herron (New York: Pocket Books, 1988). The Names Project Quilt has provided a way for people to express very personal memories as they work on an individual panel, but it has also become a community event, as the panels have been sewn together and displayed across the country.

9. See *Stress Response Syndromes,* by M. Horowitz (Northvale, N.J.: Aronson, 1986), and *The Courage to Grieve,* by Judy Tatelbaum (New York: Harper and Row, 1980).

10. According to a report by the San Francisco Department of Health, "the length of survival [of persons with AIDS] increased significantly in 1986 and 1987." *San Francisco Sentinel,* January 26, 1988.

11. Ibid.

12. Gerald Friedland, of Montefiore Medical Center in New York, and Robert Redfield, of the Walter Reed Institute of Research in Washington, D.C., were quoted at the Fourth International Conference on AIDS in Stockholm. "The Helquist Report," by Michael Helquist, *The Advocate,* August 16, 1988, p. 26.

Other AIDS resources: *Living with AIDS—A Self-Care Manual,* edited by Lang, Spiegel, and Strigle (Los Angeles: AIDS Project, 1984).

When Someone You Know Has AIDS—A Practical Guide, by L. Martelli with F. Peltz and W. Messina (New York: Crown Publishers, 1987). A thorough and helpful manual for lovers and friends.

As We Are, by Don Clark, (Boston: Alyson, 1988), describes the new sense of identity emerging in the gay community as we care for one another in the AIDS crisis.

For more on mental health issues with AIDS, see *What to Do About AIDS—Physicians and Mental Health Professionals Discuss the Issues,* edited by Leon McKusick (Berkeley: University of California Press, 1986).

The San Francisco AIDS Foundation has many AIDS resources and education materials, including the *Bulletin of Experimental Treatment for AIDS (BETA):* 333 Valencia Street, San Francisco, Calif. 94103; (415) 864-4376.

AIDS bibliographies now include hundreds of articles and books. Check your bookstores and libraries for other resources on specific topics.

Chapter 11

1. For some tips on what to look for in a gay-sensitive therapist, see *The Lavender Couch,* by Marny Hall (New York: Alyson Press, 1985).

Chapter 12

1. *The Natural Mind—A New Way of Looking at Drugs and the Higher Consciousness,* by Andrew Weil (Boston: Houghton Mifflin, 1972), p. 19.
2. Ibid., p. 31.
3. See *Drugs I: Society and Drugs,* by Richard H. Blum and Associates (San Francisco: Jossey-Bass, 1969). Among other examples, Blum contrasts the social use of alcohol in Greece with the problems it introduced to Native Americans, who had no traditional rituals for its use and whose cultures had been disrupted.
4. For a discussion of the effect of social relationships and expectations on addiction, see *The Social Controls of Non-medical Drug Use,* by Norman Zinberg and Richard Jacobson (Washington, D.C.: Interim Report to the Drug Abuse Council, Inc., 1974). For controlled opiate use among medical patients, see *Addiction and Opiates,* by Alfred R. Lindesmith (Chicago: Aldine, 1968).
5. Adapted from the Johnson Institute's training on Chemical Dependency and the Family, Minneapolis, Minnesota.
6. Ibid.
7. Some researchers question whether several adoption and twin studies demonstrate that alcoholism is a genetic disease. See *Science News* 134:74.
8. For more information on alcoholism in the gay community, see *Gay and Sober—Directions for Counseling and Treatment,* by Thomas O. Ziebold and John E. Mongeon (New York: Harrington Park Press, 1985). Also see *Accepting Ourselves—The Twelve-Step Journey of Recovery from Addiction for Gay Men and Lesbians,* by Sheppard B. Kominars (San Francisco: Harper and Row, 1989).
9. Adapted from the "Short Michigan Alcoholism Screening Test," *Journal of Studies on Alcohol* 36(1975): 117–26.
10. *"It Will Never Happen to Me,"* by Claudia Black (New York: Ballantine, 1987).
11. "A codependent person is one who has let another person's behavior affect him or her, and who is obsessed with controlling that person's behavior." *Codependent No More,* by Melody Beattie (New York: Harper/ Hazelden, 1987), p. 31.
12. *The Natural Mind,* pp. 105–107.
13. Ibid., pp. 194–95.
14. See "Ritual, Symbol and Sacrament" in *The Perennial Philosophy,* by Aldous Huxley (New York: Harper and Row, 1945).

Chapter 13

1. According to sociologists Martin P. Levine and Richard Troiden, *Journal of Sex Research,* August 1988, "the invention of sexual addiction and sexual compulsion as 'diseases' threatens the civil liberties of sexually variant peoples." It's useful to consider whether you're using a specific

behavior (such as sex, drinking, or working too hard) to ward off feelings, and not get distracted by the debate over whether it can be classified as an actual illness. See the next two notes.

2. It's important to distinguish sexual compulsion from the psychological diagnosis of "obsessive-compulsive disorder," which refers to hand-washing and other ritualistic compulsions. The sufferer generally realizes the absurd nature of these rituals, but feels compelled to complete them nonetheless. This disorder is thought to have a biological component, and in many cases responds to antidepressant medication. I am not using the word "compulsive" in this sense here. See "The Biology of Obsessions and Compulsions," by Judith L. Rapoport, in *Scientific American,* March 1989, p. 83.

3. The word "addiction" is used here in the sense of psychological habituation, not physical dependency.

4. See *Bradshaw on: The Family—A Revolutionary Way of Self-Discovery,* by John Bradshaw (Deerfield Park, Fla.: Health Communications, 1988). He describes addictive and codependent behaviors that are common among adult children from dysfunctional families (including survivors of sexual, physical, and emotional abuse, as well as alcoholic or substance-abusing families).

5. See *Sex and Love Addicts Anonymous* (Boston: The Augustine Fellowship, 1986). SLAA was formed in 1976, and has meetings in many cities. Write to: Augustine Fellowship, P. O. Box 119, New Town Branch, Boston, Mass. 12258.

6. For a thorough description of the effects of sexual abuse on male survivors, see *Victims No Longer—Men Recovering from Incest and Other Sexual Child Abuse,* by Mike Lew (New York: Nevraumont Publishing Company, 1988).

Other resources: *Love and Addiction,* by Stanton Peele with Archie Brodsky (New York: New American Library, 1978).

Looking for Love in All the Wrong Places—Overcoming Romantic and Sexual Addictions, by Jed Diamond (New York: G. P. Putnam's Sons, 1988).

Drama of the Gifted Child—How Narcissistic Parents Form and Deform the Emotional Lives of Their Talented Children, by Alice Miller (New York: Basic Books, 1981).

Chapter 14

1. The Marin (California) Domestic Violence Project calls this devastated feeling the "fatal peril."

2. Marin's program has men reenact "movies" of violent incidents, so they can pinpoint when they decide to act violently.

3. From a study by Community United Against Violence (see note 6).

4. Men Overcoming Violence has groups for gay men who batter: 3004 16th Street, San Francisco, Calif. 94114; (415) 626-6683.

5. Community United Against Violence has groups for gay men who have been battered: 514 Castro, San Francisco, Calif. 94114; (415) 864-3112. You can also get help from codependency groups or Sex and Love Addicts Anonymous.

6. This use of time out was also developed by the program in Marin.

Chapter 15

1. See the *Legal Guide* for sample contracts.

2. "Loneliness," by Robert Weiss, *Harvard Medical School Mental Health Letter,* vol. 4, no. 12 (June 1988): 4. He cites John Bowlby's identification of separation distress in children, Colin Murray Parkes's work on adult bereavement, and his own study of Parents Without Partners.

3. Ibid., p. 5. He also distinguishes between social isolation and the loneliness of "attachment deficit."

4. See *If I'm so Wonderful, Why am I Still Single?,* by Susan Page (New York: Viking, 1988), a great guide for evaluating your readiness for a relationship and devising a plan for finding one.

INDEX